Wheelchairs, Perjury and the London Marathon

Tim Marshall

Clink
Street

London | New York

Published by Clink Street Publishing 2017

Copyright © 2017

First edition.

The author asserts the moral right under the Copyright, Designs and Patents Act 1988 to be identified as the author of this work.

ISBN: 978-1-912262-57-1 paperback
978-1-912262-58-8 ebook

Preface

The idea for writing this book came to me during a prolonged stay in the high dependency unit of the Spinal Injury Centre in Middlesbrough in early 2013. As I chatted with one of the nurses, she let slip that she had once done the London Marathon, in 1983, the first year that she was allowed to run that distance, having reached the age of 18. 1983 was also the first year that wheelchairs were let in, so we swapped memories of our experiences. The idea for a book arose from that conversation, and this is the story of how the wheelchair section came about.

Thanks to Kathy for inadvertently provoking the idea in the first place (she really didn't realise what she had unleashed!); to Mick, Mark, Denise, Gerry, Jo, Gordon, Joe, Ric, Stuart, Chas and all the others whose names I have forgotten but who were part of the early struggle; to Caroline, Jon, Libora and Liz for their comments on earlier drafts; to Liz also for her more than tacit support, which resulted in the crucial contact with the GLC; and finally to Caroline again, who, when friends have (unwisely) asked about my involvement with London, has had to suffer an abbreviated version of the whole book on innumerable occasions. Text within square brackets convey my own thoughts and feelings, often after the event. Any remaining inaccuracies and faults are of course mine. I can only plead the fallibility of memory of events over 30 years ago, and that the documentary records are rather incomplete.

Hospital

In September 1972 I was climbing in the Peak District with a friend from work, on the gritstone at Birchens Edge just above the Robin Hood pub where the road from Baslow to Sheffield splits off from that to Chesterfield. Late on the Saturday afternoon I was trying to pull up a narrow crack on finger jams, but failed, and fell off, about 20 feet, landing full square on both feet and getting a compression fracture of the spine. Taken first of all to Chesterfield Royal Infirmary, two days later I was transferred to Lodge Moor Hospital in Sheffield, the regional centre for the management of spinal injuries. This was to be my home for the next eight months.

The hospital was high up on the moors at the western edge of the city, with no buildings beyond it. In the acute ward, you could hear the clip-clop of horses from the local riding school as they trotted along the roads beyond the grounds of the hospital; and, depending which way you were facing when lying in bed, you could see the helmets bobbing up and down above the dry stone walls, the sight accentuated when, as often seemed to happen that winter, the fields were covered in snow. Round to the right, and way down in a deep-cut valley, was the A57 road that came out of Sheffield, over to the Ladybower dam, and on to the Snake Pass, offering access to the high moorland of the Dark Peak. It was inviting, even if the immediate prospect of getting there was non-existent.

But the outdoors wasn't entirely out of bounds. One day I woke to a snow-covered paradise. It had snowed overnight, well over an inch, and the sky was a crystal clear blue; I decided to go out and enjoy this.. Despite the blazing sun, it was very cold as I pushed the wheelchair through an inch of snow up to the helipad at the back of the hospital, and sat there surrounded by the snow, in utter quietness, soaking in the pleasures of being outside, in the country once again. Almost everyone thought I was mad, but the ward sister – who could beat me at Scrabble, and was altogether a very impressive lady – knew, for me, what that experience was about; simply magical.

The physiotherapist assigned to me, Harry Charles, was a leading light in the hospital sports club – strictly speaking, the Spinal Injury Sports Club – so even though I was stuck in bed for the first 10 weeks, there was an early introduction to the sports side of rehabilitation. The gym, in which all the sports took place, had originally been an ordinary ward (South 2, or S 2) when the whole hospital was an isolation hospital for infectious diseases; and there was still one ward functioning as the regional infectious diseases unit. But S 2 became the gym when the Spinal Injury Unit was established there in the early 1950s.

While I was still in bed in Lodge Moor I had seen a clip on the BBC's Saturday afternoon "Grandstand" programme taken from the Paralympic Games held in Heidelberg. They showed a British athlete in a wheelchair doing what the programme called a slalom, pushing the wheelchair along a pre-set track, tipping the wheelchair onto its rear wheels to bounce up or down a step, ducking low like a limbo dancer to get under a low tape, and so on. My memory of this broadcast finished with the man in the wheelchair doing a back-wheel balance on the two rear wheels, and in my memory the wheelchair fell over backwards and the man fell out. The programme had introduced him as Philip Craven.

A few weeks later, still stuck in bed, I had a letter from France. I didn't know anyone in France; what on earth was this about? It turned out to be from the same Philip Craven, who at that time, he told me, was teaching wheel-chair basketball, and other sports too, at a rehabilitation centre at Kerpape in southern Brittany. (The connection to him was obscure: a daughter of some friends of my parents had been at university with Philip, already in a wheel-chair from a climbing accident at the age of 16. She contacted him about me, and so he wrote to me.) This was the first instance of contact with Philip that was to continue, on and off, for the next 40 years.

Once I was allowed to start getting up the gym was an obvious destination. Other than Wednesdays it was used routinely as part of the rehabilitation programme, but on Wednesday afternoons it was used by ex-patients who came up for a sort of mini sports day, when as far as possible the gym was cleared of moveable equipment to enable people to play battington (a kind of badminton but with solid rackets), table tennis, snooker and wheelchair basketball. The size of the central section of the gym, maybe 15 yards by 6, made basketball – no more than 4 a side at maximum and more usually 3 – especially exciting to watch.

It was Harry Charles (actually a Remedial Gymnast rather than a physiotherapist) who got me playing table tennis, along with his successor John Honey, just finishing his training in physiotherapy. Swimming was also sometimes on offer, very good for paralysed limbs, but I'd never been a water sort of person, had never learned to swim, and I didn't take up the pportunity then. It was Harry, though, who first aroused my interest in wheelchair sports, and who encouraged me to go to the national championships held annually at Stoke Mandeville.

My first visit there was straight after being discharged from hospital. I had supposed that going to "The Nationals", as the games were universally described, would involve a rigorous selection procedure. I had no idea what that might be, but presumably through some regional or club-based structure based on performance: were you good enough? The presumption was partly correct, in that the hospital sports club made the entry for you, including such details as sex, level of disability and which sports you were going to do; but it seemed that anyone could go, regardless of ability, provided that they were attached to an existing sports club. At that time the clubs were essentially hospital-based, and the hospitals were those with spinal injury units. So, there was "my" club – Lodge Moor Spinal Injury Sports Club – and clubs from other hospitals: Stoke Mandeville, Pinderfields (Wakefield), Southport and so on. The only exception to this that I could discover was the Scots, who came down as the Scottish Paraplegic Association, rather than from Musselburgh or Philipshill, the two hospitals in Scotland then offering specialised treatment for spinal injuries.

One memory from that first visit to Stoke was of meeting Philip Craven, but also of meeting a colleague of his from the Southport club, Gerry Kinsella, who was later to do remarkable things in setting up and running the Greenbank project on Merseyside. This was a project teaching the empowerment of people with disabilities through education, employment training and so on. At that time the Southport club was a powerhouse in UK wheelchair basketball; Philip and Gerry were both in the international squad.

Stoke, however, wasn't the only sports event for the spinal injury community. Most of the spinal units put on a day's sports event, featuring all the usual sports: basketball, bowls, table-tennis, field events, and so on. There were the Pinderfields games, the Lodge Moor games, the Southport games … These events also provided the opportunity for those aspiring to international selection for both more competition and to strut their stuff in front of the selectors, who thus had a wider range of events in which to appraise some-one's abilities. But there were occasionally events which were unique to the particular centre. At Sheffield, the last event of the day was always what was called a marathon. Of course, it wasn't anything like a marathon: it began on the outdoor basketball court, turned left along a poorly-surfaced road which ran along the back of the hospital, turned round at the end and came back along the road, and up to the helipad. There it did a 180° turn and back to the finish at the basketball court; maybe ¾ mile in total. There were usually 30 or 40 participants, and during the several years that I went to the games, the winner was always the aforementioned Gerry Kinsella, from the Southport club; this was a pointer to the future, though I didn't know it at the time.

A final memory of my first visit to Stoke was of Professor Guttmann's farewell address to the assembled athletes. This was 25 years after the first games had been held in 1948, and he lauded particularly two people – John and Gwen Buck – who had attended every National Games right from the beginning, both achieving international selection in bowls, both of them fine examples of making it in the spinal injury world through the medium of sport, and all starting at Stoke Mandeville 25 years ago. Yes, I thought, I'll be here in 25 years' time, just like they are now…

Stepping Out

It didn't quite work out like that. Becoming involved with a wheelchair basketball club from the Nottingham/Derby area, a breakaway from the original Lodge Moor club, and successive visits to the nationals, slowly opened my eyes to give a broader view. Firstly, Stoke appeared to be an organisation limited to spinal injury wheelchair users, not wheelchair users with other causes of having lost the use of their legs, or other disabilities altogether; somehow, that didn't seem quite right. (My initial understanding of the place wasn't strictly correct: the lettering across the outside of the main sports hall announced it to be "Stoke Mandeville Stadium for the Paralysed and Other Disabled". It was just that, at the time, the "Other Disabled" seemed conspicuously absent.) And secondly, many of the people I met in the sports world seemed largely to have their lives, especially their recreational lives, totally described by, even defined by, their disability. Of course, this wasn't true of everyone, and those of whom it *was* true seemed quite contented; but I didn't want such a life. I had had the good fortune of being appointed to a lectureship – more on promise than achievement, I think – in the department where I'd been working for two years before the accident. I also found a place in a hall of residence, where I eventually became an assistant warden. The job, and living in a hall of residence, however artificial in relation to "real" life, brought about a wider perspective. Disability wasn't one of my fundamental characteristics like gender or ethnicity. It was there all right, all the time, but it didn't define what or who I was.

For me, it was important to keep contact with the climbing club, the social group with whom I felt the closest affinity, and within which I'd already developed a number of good friendships which survive to this day, over 40 years later. Curiously, this had been quite easy to do when in hospital, as the club owned an old gritstone cottage barely 5 miles from the hospital, so that the ward was frequently invaded on Sunday evenings by a large group of climbers on their way back to London from a weekend away; visiting rules were quite relaxed at the time. This contact was part of the essentially outdoor recreational lifestyle which had become so important to me, and which I was determined to keep going, somehow, once out of hospital. Difficult in the first year out, it became a lot easier once I had my own transport (a van) fitted out for sleeping in, so that I could go away for whole weekends once again. Of course, going away at weekends didn't mean I actually went climbing. Whilst the others went off to the crags, I began exploring disused railway lines and forest trails, which could be found in abundance in both the Peak District and North Wales. And failing these, there was always the possibility of using minor roads.

In the mid- to late-1970s I was still involved with the Notts and Derby club, mostly for wheelchair basketball, but also from time to time for table-tennis. Local authority recreation departments would stage a day, or an afternoon, of disability sport, and invite local disabled sports clubs to take part. Thus it was that, one grey, dank, drizzly November day in a sports centre in what felt like the back of beyond – actually, the outer regions of Stoke on Trent – we arrived to play an exhibition game of basketball, and to try anything else that was going. One such was short mat bowls, which by some extraordinary luck I managed to win, and win a small cup to boot. Club members were enthusiastic for me, pointing out that if I could transfer the skills I obviously had to outdoor greens, I could easily find myself on international trips to – well, all over. The prospect didn't seem that enticing, certainly not in comparison with what I hoped – thought – the outdoors might yield, if only I could find out more. But how?

Exploring outdoor activities further came about from a completely unexpected source. The concept of Town Twinning, which took off after the Second World War, drew together cities and towns from different countries with something in common. So, for example, a fishing town on the northeast coast of Scotland might be twinned with a fishing town from Brittany and a German town from the Friesland coast. The idea was to develop knowledge and understanding of the different cultures of peoples from countries which had spent much of the last 60 years fighting each other. Over the years, Birmingham had become twinned with Lyon, Frankfurt and Leipzig (then in East Germany). Thus it was that in the autumn of 1976 a group of people from Birmingham came together to go on an informal visit to Lyon for a swimming competition, and would I like to come? As a non-swimming table-tennis player there didn't seem much point (except that a visit to Lyon would always be nice), but a table-tennis tournament was added so I was on the plane.

Attached to the group that went to Lyon, both as a general helper/carer and as a qualified ASA instructor, was someone called Sheila Dobie, who in the past had been involved with the swimming group from Stoke. Though I don't remember at all, I must have talked to her about my interest in outdoor activities, because the next thing that happened, in early 1977, was getting a letter from someone called Liz Dendy at the Sports Council. She explained that she had been given my name by Sheila Dobie, who had told her of my interest in outdoor activities. Liz went on to say that this was an area the Sports Council was interested in, and they were organising a week-long event at Plas y Brenin, the national climbing centre in North Wales, for instructors of disabled people in outdoor activities, and that they needed some disabled people to act as role models (or guinea pigs, though that term was never used in official documentation). Would I be interested in taking part? *Would* I?

New Horizons

The designated week was the first week in June 1977, Silver Jubilee week. I had to obtain permission from my head of department to be absent during term time, not so difficult then as the students were approaching exams, there was no more teaching, and I was only peripherally involved with the exams. So I was allowed to go. But I had to learn to swim first, and this was done with the help of a couple of staff from the PE department at the university. It was pretty obvious, though, that swimming was not going to be one of my favourite activities, since I hated putting my face in the water, and only ever achieved a doggy paddle on my back. But at least, if I fell into water, I would be unlikely to drown.

The weather in North Wales was awful, pouring with rain almost every day, but it didn't seem to matter. There were some indoor sessions where different people explained how their disability affected the physical requirements of an activity (canoeing, sailing, skiing etc.). Practical sessions showed how people could overcome or circumvent the limitations imposed by the disability. I spent most of the time paddling a canoe, something called a Caranoe made by Frank Goodman from Valley Canoe Products in Nottingham.

The Caranoe was different from other canoes: it was wider, had an enormously long cockpit, and had a fluted base running the length of the craft, rather like corrugated iron, though with much larger corrugations. These, and its width, gave it far greater stability than an ordinary canoe, and the size of the cockpit made it much easier to get in and out. We were, however, trained to get out of an ordinary canoe, should the need ever arise, i.e. if you capsized.

Despite the awful weather, what came to matter from that week was meeting Liz Dendy, and also Norman Croucher, a double below-knee amputee with artificial legs who had started climbing before his accident, and simply carried on developing his climbing skills afterwards. (Later, he went on to climb Cho Oyu, one of the 8000 metre peaks of the Himalayas). Norman was at that time a member of the Great Britain Sports Council, and it was he and Liz who between them had had the idea of putting on this course.

Subsequently, Liz asked me to join an advisory group at the Sports Council, on water sports for disabled people, and so I met those who had been heavily involved with developing their sport for people with a disability: Mike Hammond with water skiing (he had also done lots with snow skiing), Ken Roberts with sailing, and so on. It may also have been during the week at PyB that I met Bill Parkinson, who was the "Northern Development Officer" for the BSAD, the British Sports Association for the Disabled, which had been established by Ludwig Guttmann in 1961 to provide sports opportunities for people with a physical disability other than spinal injury. Quite what Liz thought I had to offer a group consisting of people already expert in their chosen field, to this day I don't know; but a new world beyond that of the climbing club – and Stoke Mandeville – was beginning to open up.

At around the same time, a PE student from the hall of residence, Ged Brennan, had developed an interest in outdoor activities for disabled people. She was a good canoeist, so good that she was used by the PE department of the university as one of the instructional staff on the Introduction to Outdoor Activities course which was held at the end of every summer term for all first year PE students. Ged wondered whether I might be interested in going to the university's outdoor centre by the side of Lake Coniston and spending some time canoeing, and maybe sailing too. There was, she assured me, a canoe held in the centre which, with minimal alteration (the fitting of a backrest), should be suitable. She had talked to the member of staff responsible for running the first year courses and had been given permission for me to attend one of the weeks. There was a caveat – that she wouldn't need other staff members to help with me, and that her instructional activities with the first year students wouldn't be compromised.

So off I went to Coniston, and had a wonderful week, including sailing in a GP 14 down to Peel Island – featuring as Wild Cat Island in Arthur Ransome's "Swallows and Amazons". Initially, we had no idea how best to accommodate someone like me in a GP. Ged tried strapping a plastic chair to the floor of the boat and putting me on it, but I was too tall, and had to take serious avoiding action every time the boat was put about, either tacking or gybing. Eventually we discovered that for me, the best way was to sit transversely on the floor with a foam rubber cushion underneath.

Most of the week, though, I spent canoeing (the backrest worked), including crossing the lake to Fir Island – and being capsized on the way back by a water-skier who decided to pirouette around me. With wash from the power boat and the skier coming at me from all sides I didn't stand a chance, and duly capsized in the middle of the lake. It was then that the training drummed into me at Plas y Brenin came into full force: "Don't try and get out halfway over, go right round until you are completely upside down, then lean forwards and with your hands either side of the edge of the cockpit, push backwards so that you roll forwards out of the canoe. Your life jacket will bring you to the surface from where a rescue can be carried out." And that's exactly what happened, except that dragging me into the Centre's rescue boat was a bit more difficult than rescuing an able-bodied person would have been. (As a footnote, water-skiing was subsequently banned on Coniston by the Lake District Special Planning Board, though that decision had nothing to do with my experience.)

The summer of 1977 was the first time I went to "The Internationals", the counterpart of "The Nationals", started in 1952 by Ludwig Guttmann and held every year at Stoke Mandeville, except in Olympic years when he tried to arrange for the Games to be held in the same country as the Olympics, though not necessarily in the same city. For example, in 1968 Mexico felt unable to cope with problems faced by tetraplegics at altitude, and Israel offered to host the Games instead. And in 1980, Russia stated that it didn't have any paraplegics (!) so the Games went to Arnhem. The current model, of the Paralympics following the Olympic Games in the same city, was finally adopted in the Seoul Games of 1988.

I went to Stoke as a spectator, not an athlete (I wasn't good enough). But although this was regarded as a high point, indeed the pinnacle, of wheelchair sports, or more specifically spinal injury sports, not a word could be found in the national press. The media was full of tennis (Wimbledon), cricket, bits of athletics, golf and horse racing, and even then, in high summer, football.

What was the problem? I wondered. Was it just the pressure on space in the newspapers, or that the games weren't regarded as serious sport at all? The local newspaper usually carried something, but almost invariably in the middle of the paper as a human interest story ("such brave people, overcoming adversity…"). Or was it that the games took place in a small country town some 40 miles outside London, where no one from the sports departments of national papers ever went? Was I just being naïve in expecting any coverage at all?

I wondered how the Americans fared in this regard. And how they got on with the more adventurous end of the sports and recreation "market" for disabled people. Would they be "pushing back the frontiers" or so cowed by a litigious environment that no one would ever try anything different from the standard spectrum of sports seen every year at Stoke? That first visit to the internationals provided no answers (maybe I hadn't found the right people to talk to). It may have been during this week I began to develop the idea of an entirely different approach to the reporting of disability sport: if sports reporters couldn't be bothered to visit and report on what they presumably thought was an unimportant activity, how about staging disability sports events as part of an able-bodied sports event? You could call it integration, of a sort, I supposed. At the time I had absolutely no idea of what this might entail, let alone how to bring it about; and in any case, it would surely be very different for different sports. The idea sank into the sub-conscious.

A Churchill Fellowship

Back in the hall of residence all had gone quiet, as term – indeed, the year – had finished and the students had all disappeared for the summer. The pigeon holes where their post was distributed by the hall office remained largely empty, though some post too big for the pigeon holes was simply left on top of the table below. Mass circulars were not routinely forwarded, the hall office told me, but they would wait a week or so – a student might have been passing, even in the middle of the summer vacation, and have dropped in to pick up any post – before forwarding individual letters, or throwing mass circulars away.

One day a dozen or so plastic-wrapped circulars appeared on the table. Through the plastic I could just see that they were from the Youth Hostel Association (YHA). Curiosity arose. I'd done a lot of hostelling before my accident, and I wondered what kind of information was being sent out nowadays. I picked up an envelope that had been sent to a student who had graduated and left the university altogether. Somewhere inside was an advertising panel. The Winston Churchill Memorial Trust (WCMT) had just announced its new topics for awards to be made in 1978. Amongst the topics was "Leisure and Recreational Pursuits for the Disabled". I read on, and eventually sent for an information pack.

The WCMT was established shortly after Churchill died. A large sum was raised by public appeal, and rather than build a statue (which pigeons might have no respect for) or some other physical memorial, the Trustees decided to invest the funds to produce an annual income which could then be used to finance a number of bursaries, or scholarships, for UK citizens to travel abroad to learn about some aspect of a subject which the trustees had announced as one of this year's topics. There were 8–10 topics each year (they changed every year), with 100 or so bursaries awarded in total. The trade-off for the

13

Trust was that individuals receiving a fellowship had to write a report about their travels, and show how they would implement what they had learned during their time away. In this way, it was felt, the Trust would be enhancing the development of civic activity in the country as a whole.

There were three stages to an application. You sent in an outline proposal (one paragraph only) of what you wanted to do. There was some sort of screening activity in the WCMT headquarters, as a result of which those who passed muster were invited to write a fuller proposal about what they wanted to do, where they wanted to go, how long for, and so on. A further screening process led to interviews for those who passed the second stage. And then, finally, those who succeeded in the interview were awarded a fellowship. I put together a brief outline of what I wanted to do, under the clumsy umbrella title of "Outdoor and adventure sports for the disabled, and integration with the able-bodied", and sent it off.

There was further help from people already far more deeply involved in disability sport than I was. Norman Croucher told me of a centre shortly to be opened in the Lake District which would be offering week-long residential courses in outdoor activities for disabled people. He had become a trustee, and told me when the official opening was taking place, some time in the autumn. I went, hovered in the background (I had absolutely no official status there at all), and managed to snatch a word with the newly-appointed director, Emrys Evans, about visiting the centre to see what was what: what they were going to do, how, and for whom. I arranged to visit early in the new year. And Bill Parkinson, either during the Plas y Brenin week or later, lent me a copy of an American wheelchair sports magazine "Sports 'n Spokes", which he thought might be of interest. It was. It covered the conventional range of wheelchair sports – basketball, table-tennis, ten pin bowling, and so on – but also new developments in wheelchair design, and new sports and activities tackled apparently for the first time by wheelchair users. Eventually, I took out a subscription.

In the meantime I managed to pass the first hurdle of the WCMT application process, and had to put together a fuller application. With hindsight, what I *said* I wanted to do turned out to be only partly what I ended up doing. The original idea was to attend a few of the American regional wheelchair games to see how they managed the publicity, and to go to their national games, which always seemed to be held under the aegis of the Bulova watch manufacturing and repair factory in New York. This turned out to be a no-no, for all the regional games, and their national meeting, had occurred well before the summer vacation here, realistically the only time I could find a large enough block of time free of student teaching. (It was obvious, really: the Internationals were usually in late July, so in order to select a team the American nationals had to be held earlier, and the regional events through which you qualified to attend their nationals, earlier still. This would have brought these events back to May and June, several weeks before I could get away. Thank heavens no one in the Churchill Trust seemed to have rumbled that.)

From "Sports 'n Spokes" I found an Outward Bound course being put on by the Minnesota OB School, a mixed course (able-bodied and disabled) based largely around a canoe-camping expedition in the Boundary Waters Canoe Area 50 miles north-west of Lake Superior (but whose waters, I was to discover later, drained 400 miles north to Hudson's Bay). Going on this course was part of the application, stressing a "pushing back the boundaries" of what was conventionally regarded as suitable for disabled people to undertake. A visit to the campus of the University of Illinois at Champaign-Urbana was more or less mandatory for a wheelchair user visiting the USA on a sort of study tour. Since early post-war, the campus had been developed to make it totally accessible for wheelchair users, and some of what I might find there might be useful back in Birmingham. And I proposed to start the visit by attending the American Spinal Cord Injury Association annual conference in Chicago, to make contacts and thereby fill out quite a lot of unprogrammed time in what I estimated would be a 6-week fellowship.

Rather to my surprise I was invited for an interview, late in the autumn. The visit to London, necessarily by train, started badly. At that time there was no provision for wheelchairs in the ordinary coaches, not even in first class, so it was travel in the guard's van, or don't travel at all. Well, OK, that's how it was, I knew that. But the train was late, and years before the advent of mobile phones there was no way of telling the WCMT that I was likely to arrive late. I *think* I remember phoning them from the forecourt at Euston to explain a "late arrival at...", but there was then the question of getting to the Trust offices in South Kensington. I had allowed enough time to push – it was about three miles – but the train's being late prohibited that. This was well before either buses or taxis were accessible to wheelchair users, so instead I had to use the underground – from which, of course, wheelchairs were formally banned, at least from the deep underground sections.

From previous visits to London I knew that the best way was *not* via the ostensibly most direct route using the Northern line to Leicester Square and changing to the Piccadilly (there were steps on the interchange) but instead going backwards, on the Victoria line to King's Cross–St Pancras, and changing to the Piccadilly there (the interchange was step-free). Using escalators – down at Euston – was just part of the normal way of getting about. But what the station at South Kensington was like I didn't know. It was no use asking any station officials, because of the ban on wheelchairs.

As it turned out South Kensington was partly accessible. There was a lift from the platform which deposited passengers on a sort of gantry which ran above and across all the platforms, but which left a flight of steps up to the foyer. As ever in these circumstances it was a question of nobbling a couple of passing travellers, and one station man, to carry me up the stairs. As a result of all that had gone before, I wasn't in the calmest state on reaching the Trust, and the pent-up frustration emerged during the interview; or so I thought.

Memories of the interview have become somewhat blurred. I remember talking about lack of publicity for events taking place in a small country town 40 miles outside London, and of trying to find out if they were any more successful in the publicity stakes in the USA; of my recent experience of outdoor activities, of my intended visit to the Calvert Trust in the new year, and again, of wondering if they had taken things further in the USA (the MOBS course suggested that they had); and thinking that the panel didn't seem at all impressed. But the most abiding memory concerned their last question, which was about the need to take a companion/carer with me to provide the personal care they apparently thought I needed. I regarded this idea as quite preposterous – I was entirely self-sufficient in self-care – and replied with near-scorn to the suggestion. And that was it. I left feeling very disappointed – I don't interview well, and the uncomfortable fact is that a) I know it, but b) don't seem to have found a way of dealing with it. It had been a worthwhile attempt, albeit in the end rather chastening; and I was still going to find out more about outdoor activities in the UK – or at least, England – through visiting the Calvert Trust early in the new year.

To my amazement, the interview was successful and I was awarded a fellowship, to study exactly what the clumsy title had stated. From memory, however, it was now so close to Christmas that trying to fill out the six weeks of the fellowship with a completed programme for a visit six months away – and who knew what contacts I might find at the American Spinal Cord Injury Association AGM which it might prove fruitful to follow? – had to be parked until the new year.

Derwentwater

At New Year I went north to the Lakes, and on New Year's day was in Keswick. In the main street around the Moot Hall there appeared to be a gathering of runners. Asking around it turned out that this was the first (?) New Year's Day run of its kind: along Borrowdale to Seatoller, then up over Honister and down to Buttermere, followed by a return over Newlands and via Portinscale back to Keswick. About 22 miles, someone told me, a road race but largely for fell-runners.

Having watched them leave I wandered off in the opposite direction, out of Keswick and on pavements and footpaths to Portinscale. I turned left and went along the road which wound own the western side of Derwentwater. The traffic was very light, almost non-existent. I reached a junction where one road was signposted to Grange, a small village just beyond the southern end of Derwentwater, bypassed by the runners as they made their way along Borrowdale; the other road went to Newlands and Buttermere, from where the runners would be coming back. There was a man standing at the junction, almost as though he was directing the runners to the correct road to take, with what looked like a pile of plastic water bottles; refreshments for the runners, I supposed, as they made their way back to Keswick with only a couple of miles to go.

He shouted across to me. "Hi, what are you doing here?"
"Don't worry, I haven't been on the run."
"Aye, I know, but what are you doing?"

We got talking. He was called Boyd Millen, a scouser, living in Keswick, and currently unemployed. Yes, he was a fell runner, but the reason for acting as a marshal was injury. He talked about other runs that went on locally, and in particular an annual race round Derwentwater organised by the local athletics club: almost exactly 10 miles. "You could get round in your chair, if you've pushed up here from Keswick."

"What, me? Do you reckon?"
"Yes, no problem. When do you want to do it?"

I explained that I had to visit the Calvert Trust the following day, and then back to Birmingham for work. But Easter was a possibility.

"Aye, no problem. Leave us your address and we'll sort something out."

The next day I went to the Calvert Trust and saw the accommodation block, some of the equipment they proposed to use, including kayaks, Canadian canoes and sailing dinghies, and the intended development of a local stables so that visitors to the Centre could also try horse-riding. The provision of Canadian canoes seemed to me particularly interesting. They were more difficult than a kayak for a single individual to control, though probably more stable. However, in the event of a capsize, there was no prospect of doing an Eskimo roll, which was a theoretical possibility with a kayak (though not for someone with my level of paralysis). On the other hand, with a Canadian, there was no chance of being trapped: you just fell out. Clearly, there were pros and cons of each type of canoe, though only the Canadian offered the possibility of taking a wheelchair with you – I couldn't see how it would be practical to strap a wheelchair to the deck of a kayak and still keep the thing stable. And the carrying capacity of a Canadian was vastly greater than that of a kayak. All very interesting, but it was the chance meeting with Boyd Millen that stuck in the brain.

Back to work, and in the evenings trying to flesh out remaining bits of my time in the USA. With the agreement of the director general of the WCMT I formally applied for the Outward Bound course. I was accepted, but the Trust felt it necessary to take out full insurance cover over and above that which was normal practice for Fellows going abroad. I don't remember the cost of the course, but the director general of the Trust rang me up about the cost of the insurance to cover me on the MOBS course (which naturally reduced the availability of money to fund the rest of my time in the USA): £400 for the 10 days!

Further developments: Bill Parkinson told me about someone he had met in the USA who was at the forefront of the Therapeutic Recreation movement. This had spread beyond a narrow academic focus into Parks and Recreation departments whose responsibilities included the provision of recreation facilities and activities for their local populations. A motto – "Recreation is part of being well, so why not make it a part of becoming well" – succinctly expressed the philosophy. There was a strong academic group in TR (as it was known) at the University of Missouri at Columbia, and one of the leaders was coming to the UK in the spring. One of his activities was to give a talk at a leisure centre in Birmingham. So I went to that, was introduced to the speaker, Jerry Hitzhusen, and Columbia became another stop on the summer's programme.

And then Easter came and it was back up to Keswick. On Easter Sunday I met Boyd outside the Moot Hall in spitting rain, so bad that I put my waterproofs on. And off we went, Boyd mostly in front with me following, except where there were steep downhill sections where I let the wheelchair go. The steepest climb was just after what was then the Swiss Lodore Hotel. It was a short stretch, barely 20 yards long, but was the most difficult section of the route – this way round.

We crossed over the river at Grange, where I took my waterproofs off – it had both stopped raining and got considerably warmer – had a drink, and carried on up the climb to Manesty and the superb view from the south-west corner of the lake across to Skiddaw. Contouring along the road, we reached what I didn't know of (though Boyd did): the steep zig-zag descent at Hawse End with a cattle grid across the road. I did a back-wheel balance, bounced across the grid and continued on to the junction where I'd first met Boyd. And then through Portinscale and back to Keswick. We had some food and a drink in a café, and then went our separate ways. A week or so later I had a letter from Boyd – well, it wasn't a letter at all, just a small cutting from the local newspaper, "The Keswick Reminder", which reported our trip round the lake as having taken 2 hours 23 minutes. And with the possible exception of his appearance the following year at an event to be described later on, that was the last I heard from him. But not of him: many years later in "The Cumberland News" it was reported that he had just completed a double Bob Graham round.

It never occurred to me at the time that if we had gone round Derwentwater in the opposite direction, anti-clockwise – which, after all, was the direction I was taking when I first met Boyd – the circumnavigation would have ground to a halt after only 3 miles or so, at Hawse End. I've been across cattle grids since, lots of times, but it would have been quite impossible to do so on an uphill gradient, with the road either side being about 1 in 8 (or steeper, maybe 1 in 6). And I'm not sure that the pedestrian gate alongside the cattle grid could have been negotiated by a wheelchair, not independently anyway. Such are the vagaries of trying something like this for the first time.

The fellowship was beginning to fill out. The annual meeting of the American Spinal Cord Injury Foundation would be followed by a visit to the American equivalent of Naidex, the National Aids for the Disabled Exhibition, which by then had been running in Britain for about five years. Then to Columbia, Missouri, followed immediately by the MOBS course. Any recovery needed would be spent at the University of Illinois at Champaign-Urbana (though recovery wasn't the primary purpose of the visit), but after that was a blank, except for a planned visit to a highly developed centre for disabled people in San Francisco, and a day visiting a high school in Sacramento where, according to "Sports 'n Spokes", they had an integrated sports and recreation programme for physically disabled and non-disabled children. I hoped to be able to fill in the blank 10 days using contacts made at the meeting in Chicago.

The Internationals 1978

Earlier that year I'd won the silver medal in table-tennis in my class at the Nationals, and was asked if I'd like to go to the Internationals. Five years earlier I would have jumped at the chance but now, with bigger fish to fry, I didn't exhibit much enthusiasm at the prospect, and accordingly (and rightly) wasn't selected. But I went to Stoke anyway, to see if there were any useful contacts to be made. That aspect of the visit wasn't successful, but there were a couple of features about wheelchairs which presaged developments in the near future.

At that time the fundamental rule was that you used the same wheelchair for your sport as you used in everyday life. That is, racing, basketball, table-tennis … the wheelchair was all the same. (By analogy, it would be like using your everyday shoes also for playing football, or skiing!) It is easy to see that this would curtail the costs, but at the same time it prevented the development of chairs specifically designed to address the biomechanical requirements of individual sports: what you need for racing is quite different from what you need for basketball or tennis (though wheelchair tennis was as yet unknown in Britain). The first new development I noticed was in wheelchair basketball. There were few regulations about the chairs, but the backrest had to be at least a prescribed minimum height (to avoid people with good balance sitting on top of the backrest and thereby gaining a huge advantage in height); and the footplates had to be exactly 4 inches from the ground, so you didn't run into an opponent's shins. But one of the remaining problems was getting your fingers trapped when in a melee with other chairs: squashed fingers was a well-known side-effect of the sport. Now, someone produced a simple bit of gear which reduced the risk.

The cross-bars of a wheelchair, which enable the chair to be folded, were held together by a bolt through the middle of each bar. Now, someone produced a gadget which was fitted to the cross-bars, so that when the chair was unfolded, the main wheels became splayed, outwards at the bottom and inwards at the top. The camber to the main wheels simultaneously made the chair more stable when turning quickly (highly desirable in basketball), lighter to push and turn, and also meant that you could grip the handrim of your chair without the risk of getting your fingers squashed. And you were still using the same chair as in everyday life.

The other development was in racing. At that time Stoke didn't have a race-track, but used a strip of tarmac 6 lanes wide. It ran from some metal railings across one end along a gently rising, undulating track for about 130 yards. Individual races were started at the bottom and went uphill; any downhill leg in relay races had to allow 10 yards at the bottom end so that the wheelchairs could stop before piling into the metal railings. (If this sounds extraordinarily amateurish for an event claiming to be the highest level of wheelchair sports in the world, it should be noted that it was largely built, and run, on charitable donations, and many of the staff were volunteers.)

The standard adult wheelchair had 24" wheels. Now, the Australians turned up with 26" wheels. How much more difficult it was to transfer out of, and into, the chair, when you had to lift yourself over a wheel 2" higher than normal I never found out; but the difference when racing was obvious. Slow at the start, they soon caught up the 24"-wheeled chairs everyone else used, and powered on to finish yards ahead, evidence of the mechanical advantage given by using larger wheels. And the Australians presumably managed to persuade the powers that be that their chairs were indeed the same ones that they used in everyday life.

The lessons taught by these two developments didn't go unheeded, and at some stage the generic regulations on the use of wheelchairs were abolished, with each sport being allowed to develop its own equipment as the biomechanical requirements dictated – within whatever regulations were deemed appropriate for each sport. In addition to basketball, cambered wheels are seen now in racing (slightly), and most markedly in tennis and wheelchair rugby, whilst racing allows main wheels up to 27" in diameter.

Chicago

And so to the Fellowship. The flight to Chicago was in very early August, on a jumbo. Unusually (I thought), there was tarmac loading, not through a jetway. But not being a seasoned international traveller, I couldn't really say whether this was normal or not. We were taken downstairs to a departure lounge which looked out across to where a jumbo was parked; ours, we were told. Airport staff came and ushered people onto low floor coaches which drove off towards the plane parked a few hundred yards away. I was told to wait, someone would be along. Not having anywhere else to go, I waited. And waited. And waited … After about 45 minutes someone came down and said "Oh! What are you doing here?" "Waiting to get on the Chicago plane." "Oh God…" and disappeared. There was a flurry of activity which ended with my being put on the platform of a fork lift truck and driven across the tarmac to the plane. I was lifted up to a gaping hole in the side of the plane, much wider than a single door's width, and "guarded" with an orange tape across the gap, and two powder-blue-suited air hostesses either side, laughing their socks off. The first approach was at too sharp an angle, leaving a gap of about 18" between the platform and the plane, so the driver backed off and had another go. This time he got it right, and after a bit of adjustment for height, I pushed on board and off we went.

And that, I supposed, was that. Get to Chicago, unload, meet a man from the local chapter of the American Spinal Cord Injury Association who was coming to welcome me to his city, and the conference – I was possibly the only Brit going to the conference, and therefore something of a curiosity – and off to the hotel where the conference was being held. The best-laid plans…

O'Hare airport in Chicago was utterly chaotic. The usual rule for wheelchair users when flying was, I came to discover, first on, last off, so by the time I reached the arrival lounge the chaos was in full flight, so to speak. The poor British Airways rep. was trying to cope (and not very successfully, it seemed) with a plane-load of passengers, one-third of whom had had had their baggage left behind in London; including my wheelchair. This looked as though it might be a problem: the airport authorities put me in an airport chair, but wouldn't allow me to take it outside the terminal building. Once through immigration and customs, though, I was able to meet the man from the conference – what a lucky break that was! – and he rushed off home to bring me his spare chair, which I used for two days before my own chair reappeared, just left in the hotel room with no explanation or apology.

The next morning I was at the front desk of the hotel waiting to ask about changing some travellers' cheques when someone slapped me on the back from behind. "Hiya, you one of our guys?"

Marathons

At my grammar school in the 1950s we were taught Latin, but not Greek, which I don't think was available to anyone (interestingly, Russian was, though only as a 6th form option). And though I remember absolutely nothing about the History syllabus in the first 3 years, the O-level syllabus was on Modern European History from the French Revolution onwards; nothing about Greek or Roman history at all. So what little I knew about Greek history was picked up from...who knows where? Wasn't there something of a dust-up between Athens and Sparta at some time? And weren't the Greeks always being threatened by the Persians? Wasn't there a battle between them somewhere, sometime? Oh yes, that was the battle of Marathon, wasn't it? When someone ran to Athens bringing news of a great victory for the Greeks, against overwhelming odds, and then died? Bit of a short straw, really.

The wars between Greece and Persia went on for almost two generations, 492 to 449 BC. In fact, the Persians had already occupied a number of Greek islands as well as Greek cities on the mainland of Asia Minor, or what we now call Turkey. Of course, this wasn't Greece as we understand it today, a single political entity, but, rather, a collection of separate self-governing city-states which had cultural connections through, amongst other matters, the language, participation in the ancient Olympic Games – and resistance to incursion by a foreign power, namely Persia.

What is clear is that the first Persian invasion of the Greek mainland took place in 490 BC, and in effect it ended with the defeat of the Persians at the Battle of Marathon. There are various versions of what happened, both before and after: that Pheidippides ran from Athens to Sparta (140 miles!) to seek military help; that he ran from Marathon to Athens carrying news of the victory; that after the battle the Greek army marched the 25 miles to Athens to see the Persian fleet sailing away; and so on. Whatever the exact truth of these (and other) accounts, what matters for our purposes is the legend which has come down to us: someone, whom history has named Pheidippides, did run from the battle of Marathon to Athens carrying news of the victory, uttered the words "We were victorious" and then died, presumably from exhaustion.

The relevance of this is that when the newly-formed International Olympic Committee was looking for events to include in the first Olympic Games of the modern era, at Athens in 1896, someone suggested recreating the heroic run of Pheidippides and having a race from Marathon to Athens. Because of the starting point, the race was called a marathon. There were only 15 runners, but as luck would have it (for the organisers) the race was won by a Greek shepherd, Spyridon Louis, simultaneously establishing the event *per se*, and its popularity.

There is nothing much to be said about either the Paris Games in 1900 – held there to honour Pierre de Coubertin, who had had the idea for the Olympic Games in the first place – or those in St Louis in 1904; but the London Games in 1908 have come to be remembered for two matters. The Games were held at the White City stadium in West London, and although the marathon distance had been set at 26 miles, it was due to finish as the runners entered the stadium. At the request of Queen Alexandra, the finishing line was extended by 385 yards so that the finish of the race would be in front of the royal box. The length of the race was finally standardised in 1921 at the London distance, 26 miles 385 yards. The second matter for which the London race is remembered is, of course, the Italian Dorando Pietri, who was staggering towards the finish line but was wobbling off the course. He was helped across the finish line by concerned officials, but was subsequently disqualified precisely for having been given external assistance.

In 1894, the civic leaders in the two New England states of Massachusetts and Maine decided to institute a public holiday, to be called Patriot's Day, to commemorate the War of Independence battles at Lexington and Concord in 1775. They wanted some event to mark this day, and two years later, noting the success of the Athens marathon, decided to hold a marathon of their own, in Boston. The first race was in 1897, over a distance of 24.5 miles, on April 19th, which date was used for the next 72 years until Patriot's Day was moved in 1969 to the third Monday in April; the race has remained there ever since. The race was extended to 26 miles 385 yards in 1924, to fit in with the IAAF rules standardising the distance in 1921. The extension of the distance also made it possible to position the finishing line in downtown Boston.

The IAAF was founded in 1912, but at that time dealt only with athletics for men. The Federation Sportive Feminine International (FSFI) existed between 1921 and 1936, at which point it merged with the IAAF, which then accepted the records of the FSFI. Athletics events for women (and men) were organised at local, that is to say, national, level. An 800 metre world record for women was recognised as early as 1922, in which year the first British title (over 880 yards, or half a mile) was awarded; but the USA didn't award its first title at this distance until 1927, only a year before the metric distance appeared in the Olympic Games for the first time. 1928 was the first year women were allowed to race at the Olympics at all, with 100 metres being the other distance contested. Curiously, the 800 metre didn't reappear until Rome in 1960, whilst the first women's Olympic marathon was in 1984 at Los Angeles.

This, however, is getting ahead of things. Following the announcement in 1896 of the intention to hold a marathon race as part of the Olympic Games, in March of that year Stavatis Rovithi (a woman) ran the length of the proposed course; and a month later, another woman, Melpomene, presented herself at the start of the Olympic race but was prevented from starting. So she ran anyway, running along the side of the course and finishing in about 4½ hours, 90 minutes behind Spiridon Louis. In 1918 Marie-Louise Ledrun completed the Paris marathon in 5h 40 m. However, the IAAF recognises Violet Percy as the first, properly-timed, female marathon runner, in 3h 40m 22s, in 1926.

Subsequent records of women's achievements over the distance are patchily reported. Merry Lepper ran 3.37.07 in October 1963, while in 1966 Roberta Gibb attempted to enter Boston officially. Amongst other long-distance running achievements she had already successfully completed a trans-America run, which rather debunked the official statement that "women are not physiologically capable of running a marathon". Her application to take part was refused, but she ran the course anyway, finishing in 3.21.25, within the top one-third of all the finishing times. The organisers paid only minimal attention to her since she was an unofficial participant and therefore, officially, nothing to do with them.

However, the following year Kathy Switzer submitted an entry for Boston, under the name "K V Switzer". At that time, for runners unknown to the organisers, there was a pre-race medical. Switzer's coach went along with a health certificate asserting his (actually, her – but with initials instead of a name, who could tell?) fitness to run the distance; "he" was assigned race number 261.

Only two miles into the race officials realised that a woman had somehow inveigled her way into their men-only race, and they set about trying to stop her. The whole story is entertainingly recounted in Kathy's own words on the world wide web, where you can read about how matters developed from scratch, so to speak, complete with photographs of the attempted exclusion. Briefly, a couple of officials tried to pull her off the course, or at least to tear off the official entry number from her vest. They were prevented from doing so by members of Kathy's own running club (from Syracuse University), who were prepared precisely for this sort of attack. In short, the officials lost, and Kathy finished in 4h 20m. Interestingly, Roberta Gibb ran the race again, again unofficially, and despite being forced off the course shortly before the finishing line, managed to do 3.27.17, slower than her time the previous year, but almost an hour faster than Kathy.

Curiously, there was a logic behind the officials' attempt to remove her number. At the time the prevailing rule of the IAAF was that men and women could not take part in the same race; and that if a woman was doing so it meant that the whole race would be nullified, including the times recorded by all the men. So removing her number was the simplest way of trying to demonstrate that, actually, she wasn't part of their race.

As may be imagined, these events caused something of a furore in athletics circles, particularly in America. But the reaction was not quite what you might think. Rather than adopting a liberal, open-minded approach, recognising that previous attitudes to women's distance running was perhaps outdated, the authorities went the other way completely. The American Amateur

Athletic Union (AAU) announced a complete ban on women running marathons, on two grounds: that their existing rules banned women from competing at distances over 1½ miles (roughly, 2500 metres), and that the same rules also forbade men and women taking part in the same race. (A few years later we shall encounter exactly the same argument with respect to wheelchairs; *plus ça change...*). Four years later, in 1971, an Australian woman, Adrienne Beames, ran the first known time for a marathon by a woman in under 3 hours, in 2.46.30. Whether alerted by her time, or for other reasons (I have been unable to find out), it seems likely that the IAAF changed its hard-line stance for road-racing, at least in terms of participation though not direct competition, and the following year, in 1972, the AAU reversed its earlier decision and formally allowed women to compete over the marathon distance; Boston complied immediately.

In 1970 a "Vietnam vet", Eugene Roberts, who had lost both legs in the war, asked the Boston organisers if he could do the race in a wheelchair. They didn't give him an official entry number, but he was allowed to start a short time in advance of the main race. (In the light of what came later over here, that's a far-sighted view of things, curiously at variance with the same organiser's concurrent attitude towards women.) He finished in something over 6 hours, an inordinately long time by anyone's reckoning, but at least he finished. Then in 1975 someone called Bobby Hall wrote to the Boston organisers asking if *he* could enter the race in a wheelchair. The immediate reaction of the Boston hierarchy is not known but, perhaps mindful of the difficulties they had got into over the Kathy Switzer affair a few years earlier, and of the opprobrium then heaped on them, and the (by then) changed attitudes towards women, there was a cautious acceptance of his application. Probably he was allowed to start at the front – I haven't been able to find out – but Boston said that if he completed the course in under 3 hours they would give him a special award. This was back in the days when, under the rules promulgated by Stoke Mandeville, your sports wheelchair had to be the same as your everyday chair, so 3 hours would have been an all-but-impossible target. However, Stoke – that is the International Stoke Mandeville Wheelchair Games Federation (ISMWGF) – had no position on road-racing: it simply wasn't part of the canon of sports activities over which they claimed any jurisdiction.

If you look at the snippets of video-tape that still exist on the web, you can see that Bobby's chair, though not at all like the high-speed techno-machines of today, is visually rather different from what we were all trundling around in at the time. Though the wheels look as though they were 24 inches, the frame appears to be made of lightweight alloy, the seat is much lower than on an ordinary chair, the wheels have a slight camber and the hand-rims are smaller than was normal at the time. These features would have enabled a much faster time than would otherwise have been possible, and resulted in a time of 2h 58m, still a respectable time a few years later until the design of racing wheelchairs simply took off, and times dropped accordingly.

The Fellowship

The man who clapped me on the shoulder was called Peter – Pete – and he was from the New England chapter of the Spinal Cord Injury Foundation (who were in Chicago in large numbers). He had been on the organising committee for the wheelchair section of the Boston Marathon earlier that year, and wondered whether I had been one of the entrants – seen from behind, in the crush of a hotel foyer, and with the SCI group using the hotel for their annual conference, I could well have been. I assured him that I had never been anywhere near Boston, but encouraged him to tell me more.

That April there had been 18 entrants in the wheelchair race – I forgot to ask if any, or how many, were women – and they started 18 minutes ahead of the foot-race. The winner finished in 2h 26m 59s, two minutes ahead of the leading runner. Pete had been on the "milk float" – or the American equivalent – which filmed the whole event, and which was transmitted live as the local TV station saw fit. As a model of integration this was amazing: a "disabled" event taking place at the same time and place as the equivalent able-bodied event, with as much publicity as you could reasonably expect; I couldn't see how, for this particular sport, you could improve on it. Something for the future, I thought.

One other matter of significance to a Brit: the "Chicago Sun-Times", one of the local newspapers, had on its front page a couple of column-inches headed by the following: "British political leader arrested, charged with conspiracy to murder". It was the start of what became known as the Jeremy Thorpe affair.

The rest of the conference can be passed over in a hurry. Like many such meetings there was a curate's egg aspect to it, but for me the most important encounter was with the head of the Spinal Injury Centre at Craig Hospital,

Denver, in Colorado. At the time Craig Hospital was regarded as one of, if not the, best units of its kind in the country, with a large and flourishing Therapeutic Recreation department. When I mentioned to other delegates that I was to visit Craig, they rolled their eyes and uttered sounds of both approval and envy. As I had some spare time to fill on the Fellowship, the director was happy for me to spend a few days in his centre in early September.

The next stop was at Columbia, Missouri, to look at Therapeutic Recreation, with particular reference to how people with a disability were included in the programmes run jointly by the university and the city council. Apart from being mistaken by the college president (the equivalent of a vice-chancellor here) for a new, overseas, post-graduate student, the main memory was of hearing about someone called Jeff Minnebraker who had been experimenting with altering his wheelchair. His particular contribution was the invention of the axle plate. Hitherto, the rear wheels of the most commonly-used wheelchairs were fixed to the chair by screwing the axle-bolt through a housing in the upright stem post at the back of the chair. The invention of the quick-release axle meant that by pressing a pin in the middle of the wheel, you could release the whole wheel and its axle as one unit, which could therefore easily be replaced; very important if you had developed a puncture playing basketball, for example. But more than that: if you had an array of holes to receive the wheel and its axle, you could choose where to put the axle-bolt, according to the bio-mechanical requirements of the sport you were doing. This was eventually accepted as being within the letter of the Stoke rules, and so was embraced as part of the general guidelines for wheelchairs in sport. Lastly, and probably more important than any of the above, by moving the axle forwards on the axle-plate, the chair became much lighter to push, facilitating a back-wheel balance and so making bouncing up and down kerbs and single steps much easier or everyone. To my regret I never met Jeff. He founded the Quadra company to make and sell wheelchairs, and was one of the earliest proponents of wheelchair tennis, which I first came across a few weeks later in San Jose.

From Columbia, I flew via Chicago to Duluth for the Outward Bound course in Minnesota. The course was the hardest thing I've ever done, before or since. We went out in groups of two or three aluminium Canadian canoes, into which was piled all the equipment needed for five days by six or nine people: food, cooking equipment, wheelchairs, personal gear, tents and so on. We moved from the base across a lake to a pre-designated campsite which consisted of a flattened area with a couple of seats or benches, a metal cooking grid and, somewhere back in the woods, a long-drop wooden toilet.

Between campsites we either paddled or pushed along rough woodland tracks. There were two wheelchairs per group, and all the equipment, and the canoes, had to be carried along the tracks between landing and launching points. Very often the terrain was so rough that the wheelchairs, including their occupants, needed man-handling over the tracks too. I felt at the time that too much was expected of the able-bods in the group: to move across a track from a landing to the next launching often required them to make three complete round trips: once to carry the canoes, once to carry all the food and equipment, and once to assist the wheelies as well. All too often there wasn't much that the wheelies could do to help, and I felt pretty useless for much of the time.

Once back at the base, the course was completed with a seven-mile trot along forest tracks, ending on a pontoon stretching out into the lake, from which all the course participants were ceremonially thrown by the centre staff into the lake; we were required to wear life-jackets! I enjoyed this a lot (the run through the woods, not so much being thrown in the lake): I was doing something I was familiar with, and didn't depend on others to make any progress. And there was one useful contact made in Minnesota: someone called Jim Covino, who had done the same course the year before, and was back advising the school on various aspects of the course. He was from the west coast, San Jose, so we arranged that I would stay with him when I got over there.

Then to Champaign-Urbana, where both I and my wheelchair had to be patched up. I had scraped some skin off, and the wheelchair frame was cracked as a result of the rough terrain it had been dragged over on the portages. This was a useful resting-point before going to Denver and Craig Hospital, of which there were three main memories. The staff had taken late-stage rehab patients away for two days "camping", American style, in huts out in the countryside. I was lucky enough to be allowed to sit in on their staff de-brief, which was eye-opening in its frankness, and in particular over the widespread "confession" that, although they were working day in and day out with some severely-disabled people, they simply hadn't realised just how hard it was to be with them for 24 hours a day … and the effect this must have on the family who, after discharge, would be doing all the caring.

The other two memories concern equipment. Firstly, I was shown a "pulk", a Norwegian sledge made from glass fibre, with a back-rest and a foam rubber cushion, on/in which the wheelchair user sat and pushed him/herself about using cut-down cross-country ski sticks. For use in the winter only, of course – there was no snow in Denver in August – but in the winter … Secondly, they had something they called Cyclops, a hand-powered bicycle. This was a bicycle with three wheels, one at the front and two at the back. Instead of a saddle to sit on, as in an ordinary bike, it had a seat and back-rest; and instead of pedals and a chain-ring at the front, with gears attached to the rear wheel, it had crank-handles worked by your arms, and gears attached to the front wheel, operated by levers attached to the front steering column.

I never found out if it was their own invention quite out of the blue, or whether a local bike retailer with connections to the hospital had suggested it and they had worked on the idea together; or whether they had simply imported Cyclops from somewhere else in the country. Within my limited experience, though, it was something completely original, so of course, with encouragement from the staff, I had a go. Transferring across to the seat was OK, and the seat itself had a lap-diagonal safety belt. The seat was roughly at the same height as the wheelchair seat, and the crank-handles were within easy reach at chest height. But it was very hard work to pedal it, mostly, I think, because the gearing was too high, but that was easily altered.

The other reason it was such hard work was because, whereas on an ordinary push-bike you pedal right and left alternately with your legs whilst steering with your arms, on the handbike (as they came to be called) you both cranked and steered with your arms. And the alternating motion of the arms induced a sort of side-to-side rocking which tended to make the rider, probably paralysed from the waist down, increasingly unstable. Nevertheless, it was an imaginative development, one which subsequently has become extremely popular as a recreational activity amongst wheelchair users. And nowadays, symmetrical cranking is standard.

Off to the west coast, meeting and staying with Jim Covino, who introduced me to the principal of his Community College (who did *not* mistake me for being a new, overseas, post-graduate student!), and also to the game, new to me, and something I had not yet seen in the pages of "Sports 'n Spokes", wheelchair tennis. This was pretty simple, really: all the normal rules of tennis applied, but you were allowed two bounces rather than one. Jim was the college champion, but it gave me a kick to beat him in only two sets. The other abiding memory was of the inordinate amount of time spent retrieving balls that had finished either in the net, or behind the baseline, or off the sides (we played on a two-court terrain, so there was often a long way to go to retrieve a ball). Jim had hoped to introduce me to a friend of his, Pete Axelson, who was a paraplegic and an engineer from Stanford University, whose inventions of equipment seemed to turn up several times a year in "Sports 'n Spokes", but he wasn't around, so this was another meeting which never happened.

Looking back on what I had experienced so far, a couple of things became clear. Firstly, the Americans were more than willing to push the boat out and challenge a cushioned life-style for wheelchair users: "You can do more than you think you can". And secondly, they were imaginative in inventing equipment, or altering rules, to make a wider range of recreational activities accessible to wheelchair users; whether you wanted to go there was up to you.

A short stay in San Francisco, including a visit to the Luther Burbank High School in Sacramento to look at the integrated sports programme (it wasn't really, at least not the bit I saw), and a crossing of the Golden Gate bridge (at the northern end of which there was a sign at the start of an exit ramp saying "Wheelchairs only" – I thoroughly disapproved!), saw the end of the first part of the Fellowship. Almost. The inaugural San Francisco marathon was much advertised around the city, and I very much wanted to have a go – but it was to take place a week after I was supposed to return, alas.

There were two matters which seemed almost mirror images of events in Chicago and Heathrow over six weeks earlier. Firstly, the front page of the "San Francisco Examiner" had a small paragraph headed "Smallpox in Birmingham, England". Reading further, it revealed that a technician working in the Medical School of the university had contracted smallpox and died from the disease. The Medical School was exactly where I worked: it was going to be an interesting return. (A few days later, on returning to work, there was a notice stuck on every external door: "No-one may enter this building except those who work in here or who have business in here". That didn't seem to exclude many people: why would you try to come in if you didn't have any business to do? Was it meant to put off journalists, who of all people might think they had business in there? But that's another story.)

Secondly, and of rather greater importance to my immediate situation, there was a sort of mirror image of the trouble I'd had at Heathrow. I'd presented myself at the Pan Am check-in desk and they did all the usual stuff, including giving me a boarding card – and then, 20 minutes before departure time, came and told me I wouldn't be allowed on board. The booking had been made weeks earlier by the Churchill Trust, and they had told the airline I was a wheelchair user, but there was no calling on them for assistance at this stage. Pan Am were adamant – they wouldn't let me board without a designated carer who would look after me should the need arise. Eventually, one of the staff found an Englishman on the flight who was willing to take on the rather non-specific role of carer, and I was allowed on; I didn't have to call on him during the flight. I did, though, take some Pan Am writing paper, in the pocket of the seat in front of mine, intending to write to Pan Am with a copy to the Federal Aviation Administration, complaining about the company's policy, but never got round to it (unusual, for me).

Derwentwater For Everyone

The first part of the Fellowship was now over. The Trust took as axiomatic that you would write a report on where you went and what you did (and you weren't invited to the medal ceremony in London until you had done this); and explain how you were going to implement whatever had arisen from your trip. Writing the report took far longer than it should have done, and it wasn't until November of the following year that I submitted mine. By then, I'd already got going on a number of projects arising directly from the trip.

Still mindful of the example of the Boston Marathon, I argued (to myself) that perhaps the best way of bringing such an idea to notice in the UK was to *do* a marathon. At that stage in this country, marathoning wasn't a participation sport in the way it became very shortly afterwards, stimulated by the example of the first London race in 1981. It was an activity reserved very much for dedicated club runners, and the Amateur Athletic Association (AAA) expected all runners to be affiliated to them through membership of one of the athletics clubs – Birchfield Harriers, Coventry Godiva Harriers, and so on – which were widespread throughout the country.

At the time, probably the best-known marathon in this country was the Polytechnic Marathon, from Windsor to London; but it was the wrong time of year to tilt at that. Although I wasn't a member of any athletics club, I wrote to the organisers of both the Harlow and Barnsley marathons (Liz Dendy had found out for me what were probably the only two remaining marathons before Christmas) explaining what I'd found in the States, and asking if I could enter their race. Both said yes.

I was already pushing about two miles a day up to work and back, never mind anything extra if I went away for a weekend; but I decided I needed to be a lot fitter. So, taking no advice, I started doing extra pushing, coming back to the hall of residence for lunch, and thus doubling up the daily mileage. With no attempt at warming up first (how stupid can you get?) it wasn't long before I twinged something in my right shoulder; and though I'd read or heard somewhere that you could often run through a minor injury of this kind, attempting to do so just made it worse. Despite getting to a sports injury clinic and receiving a number of injections intended to alleviate the problem, things went the opposite way and it got worse. Dreams of a possible first wheelchair marathon in this country faded rapidly.

Nevertheless, having applied to, and been accepted by, the organisers of two marathons, I felt honour-bound to turn up and explain my non-participation. For Harlow, I took a young man from Birmingham, Mark Agar, who had come along to a session in one of the university gyms that I'd managed to book for practising basketball skills; he was now also coming along to the matches played by the Notts and Derby club. He started, a few minutes ahead of the runners, but had to give up after about 14 miles, worn out. While he was out on the course, someone approached me, identified himself as from "The Daily Mirror" (how often did the Mirror cover an event like the Harlow marathon, I wondered?) and asked me if I knew Tim Marshall. Rather embarrassed, I admitted to *being* Tim Marshall, and we had a brief conversation about wheelchair marathons in general, and my abortive attempt to do this one. We beat a retreat back to Birmingham, and I went to Barnsley on my own. And apart from talking with a local newspaper reporter, it was much the same story. A far from glorious chapter in putting into practice one of the things I'd found in the USA had, for the moment at least, ended in ignominy.

Meanwhile, Bill Parkinson had invited me north from time to time to give talks on disability sport in general, and outdoor and adventure sports in particular, to various groups of people he was working with – sports development officers, policy makers in local authorities, and so on. It must have been on one of these occasions that I floated to him the idea of a non-competitive "round Derwentwater" event some time in the spring of 1979. He took it away, and came back to me a few days later saying "Yes". So he worked on this for the next few months and I sat back and waited.

In March 1979 I received a letter beginning thus: "Dear Mr Marshall, My name is Victoria [*I can't remember her surname*] and I am in charge of organising the refreshments for the "Round Derwentwater" event on Sunday" (she gave the date, which I don't remember either, but it was in late March or April). She went on to explain that she was in the 6th form at Keswick School, and she set out precisely what would be provided, from when in the morning, until when, and for how many people. It seemed that Bill had managed to pull in not just Keswick School, or at least the 6th form, but the police, local voluntary organisations, people from the local athletics club, and so on. This was going to be some event, rather larger than I had expected.

It had been made clear in the publicity about the day that it wasn't a competitive event; that you could start at any time after 10 o'clock; that you didn't have to go the whole way round, but could instead go down the east side of the lake (in my view, much the less interesting side scenically speaking) and from Grange, just beyond the southern tip of the lake, be driven back to the school; or, you could be driven down to Grange and make your own way along the road on the western side of the lake (which included the superb views across the lake and over to Skiddaw); or you could go the whole way round, with or without any assistance.

I have three main memories of the day, apart from the generally miserable weather – cool, cloudy, spitting with rain, and pretty unpleasant. Lots of local people turned up, no doubt curious to see what was going on – very different at any rate from an ordinary fell-running event. Amongst this group was Lady Rochdale, who was one of the driving forces behind establishing the Calvert Trust. Sixty-three people turned up to participate, and though I can't now remember how many did the whole circuit, it was in the 20s or 30s. One of these was a young lad from the North-East, where many of the 63 came from, who used callipers and crutches for walking, and who arrived back at the school absolutely soaked after several hours on the road, grinning from ear to ear. And then, finally, late in the day, Gerry Kinsella turned up, and shot off down towards Grange at a speed which the motorbike policeman who accompanied him later said was extraordinary. The 6th formers directing people to turn right over the bridge at Grange made similar comments, whilst the boys who had been detailed to help people over or around the cattle grid at Hawse End were astonished at Gerry's flicking the wheelchair onto a back-wheel balance and

bouncing across the grid at high speed. He completed the route in what probably remains the fastest circuit ever recorded, 1 hour 28 minutes.

Afterwards, everyone agreed it had been a great success, and they were happy
to do it again next year, so a provisional date for 1980 was set, with Bill P.
being the liaison between the school, the police, other disability sports events
already timetabled in, and so on. The local press gave a good write-up, so that
augured well. And finally, weeks later, I was told that the event had had the
very unexpected consequence of drawing together disabled people from the
locality into forming the Allerdale Association for the Disabled, to act as a
pressure group campaigning for improved provision of services and facilities
for disabled people in the Allerdale area.

I was still hampered by my injured shoulder, treatment for which seemed to
be going nowhere; so I parked that and began to look for other opportunities.
In September 1979 some friends who were sailors told me about a weekend
conference which was to be held at the Calvert Trust on the last weekend in
October, about sailing for disabled people; I thought I'd give it a go.

The weather was glorious, though most of the time was spent indoors on a
"chalk and talk" type of programme. But on the upper floor of an old barn
there was the prototype of a new sailing boat for disabled people, called a
Challenger. This was a tri-maran with a central hull with a cockpit in which
the helmsman sat, and two sponsons, or floats, either side, which provided
lateral stability to stop the craft capsizing. The floats and the main hull were
connected by thick metal cross-beams. The mast was towards the front of
the main hull, and the controls – the main sheet, the tiller and the cord for
dropping and raising the rudder, were all arranged so as to be in front of the
helmsman. (Later refinements added cockpit controls of the Cunningham
and the kicking strap.) The cockpit could take a plastic chair (without its legs)
if you needed some back support, and you could put a cushion on the floor
if you needed a padded seat.

There was no opportunity to try the thing on water, but at this stage the
RYA Seamanship Foundation (who had sponsored the design and construc-
tion) and its director, Douglas Hurndall, were interested in seeing how easy
it was for disabled people of various kinds to get in and out of the cockpit.

Acknowledging the artificiality of getting into the craft on a solid surface rather than the more wobbly environment of water, I hopped in. Douglas then pulled on the main sheet to bring the boom across, as though you were tacking or gybing on water – and the boom hit my head. So my contribution to the design/development of the boat was to have the angle of the boom raised, along with some minor adjustment to the design of the sail to compensate for the loss of sail area which raising the boom made inevitable. The following year, when a new sailing club was established on a reservoir in the west of Birmingham, I was able to persuade the club to acquire one of the tri-marans (at no cost to the club), and began learning how to sail.

After the success of Derwentwater I began thinking about doing something on the same lines but more local to Birmingham. The regional branch of BSAD was quite keen, and at the time were involved with establishing a new disabled sports club based on a sports centre in the north of the city, Wyndley Leisure Centre. There was interest, too, from the about-to-retire head teacher of a local special school for children with a physical handicap, Ivor Mitchell, and later on from his successor, Colin Grantham. The local Lions Club was also involved, and brought a large dose of enthusiasm to the day in addition to providing sponsorship, in the form of sports equipment for the clubs of winning participants.

The main organisers were BSAD, but as with the Derwentwater affair, getting other local organisations involved in what at the time was something of a novel development, seemed to be the key. The event was advertised nationally, and drew about 50 entrants who were divided into two groups, juniors and seniors. The senior race was, I think, 4 laps with a total distance of 7 miles; the junior race was shorter, though I don't remember whether it was 2 or 3 laps. At any event, there was a lot of interest – we were on the cusp of the explosion of mass fun-running – and it was reported in the local paper under the heading "Wheelchair Brands Hatch at Sutton Park". The event ran for 5 years, 1980–1984, by which time there were hundreds of running races all over the country which welcomed wheelchairs as an extra section to their event, and the need for special wheelchair-only events seemed to have run its course. Even by 1980, however, other things were underway.

Interlude

I wondered whether it might be possible to develop a canoe-camping course in Britain of the kind that I had done in Minnesota. There was nowhere in Britain which offered quite the same possibilities as the Boundary Waters Canoe Area, though parts of Scotland looked promising, especially the west coast. Chewing this idea over with Bill Parkinson, we agreed that we would each find a couple of interested people, for a 1-week journey starting and finishing at Ballachulish just south of Fort William. The base would be the Forestry Commission campsite at Glencoe, which I knew from the previous summer (1979) had a wheelchair loo. The intended route was to be from Ballachulish out into Loch Linnhe, and down to Lismore Island. From there we would cross back to the mainland, and approach the mouth of Loch Etive where there were some well-known overfalls, the Falls of Lora, which we reckoned we should be able to paddle up and into Loch Etive at a flood tide. From the head of Loch Etive the intention was to send a couple of people overland on foot back to Glencoe and Ballachulish to bring the vehicles round to pick up people, canoes and other equipment, and reassemble on the campsite before finally returning south.

We needed people, canoes, tents and other equipment. I managed to interest a couple of students from the hall of residence, one a PE student (Anne) and the other, Josh, who had worked for a children's adventure holiday company and from which he was able to borrow a large, old Canadian canoe – that would sort carrying the wheelchair, at least. The father of another student offered – or was offered by his son – to make a roof-rack for my van to carry canoes on (Bill already had his own roof-rack), and the father of yet another student loaned the family Canadian canoe, which would, however, have to be collected from the family country cottage somewhere in south Argyll. Bill came up with another student, his girl friend and a kayak. Somehow I had acquired on long-term loan (which lasted until about 1984) a Caranoe loaned to BSAD by Frank Goodman from Valley Canoe Products at Nottingham. The bits assembled gradually, my part being completed when I collected Josh and Anne from a party at Ilkley and drove overnight to pick up the Canadian canoe from south Argyll the next morning. From there we inspected the Falls of Lora – they didn't seem too terrifying – and on to the Glencoe campsite where Bill and crew arrived a few hours later.

The first thing to do the next morning was to find out how strong a canoeing party we were, who should paddle with whom, and so on. So we took off to paddle down the river in Glen Nevis to find out. Pretty soon we realised that the trip as originally envisaged was absurdly optimistic, with the most likely outcome being a rapid capsize sending all gear but the wheelchair – which would have been tied in to the big Canadian – to the bottom of Loch Leven, or Loch Linnhe if we'd lasted that far … Nobody came to any harm in Glen Nevis, though I was capsized out of the Caranoe by Bill who was following too closely in one of the Canadians. So we beat a retreat back to the campsite to dry out, and make some other plans.

We ended up with a series of day excursions: paddling down Loch Leven from Kinlochleven to Glencoe and back again; an intended jaunt from Port Appin to Lismore Island was pulled when the wind and the waves got up and I got frightened, so we retreated to paddling round Castle Stalker at high tide (the wind dropped as quickly as it had risen); a short excursion on Loch Lochy; hiring a couple of dinghies from a local outdoor centre and frolicking around where the wind blasting down Glencoe met that coming up Loch Leven; a day off at the annual Glenfinnan Highland Games (a wonderful experience); and finally, on our way south, paddling from Grange in Borrowdale across Derwentwater and down the River Greta into Bassenthwaite to the Calvert Trust base by the side of the lake (with their permission, of course). So, although what we achieved was nothing like what was intended, it turned out to be quite a stretching week.

I had an idea for a longer, more demanding, canoe-camping circuit, starting at Fort William, paddling down Loch Linnhe as far as Inversanda on the west side of the loch and portaging across to Loch Sunart; paddling down the loch to Salen; portaging to Acharacle at the foot of Loch Shiel; paddling up to Glenfinnan; portaging to Kinlocheil; and, finally, paddling back to Fort

William. In practice, the portages here would be so long that you'd need a land party with vehicles to transport people and gear between landing and launching points. Had our trip worked as planned, I'd have approached the Outward Bound school on Loch Eil with the second idea; as it was, I kept my head down and this is the first time that the idea has seen the light of day – and, probably, the last. As far as canoeing expeditions were to go, for the time being that was that.

Chris Brasher and John Disley

Chris Brasher and John Disley were two runners who became prominent in the 1950s; both were also climbers. Brasher went to Rugby School and thence to St John's College, Cambridge. In 1951 he won the 5000 metres at the World Student Games, and finished second in the 3000 metres steeplechase (this is a *very* unusual combination, one that I doubt has ever been seen in any major athletics event – Europeans, Worlds or Olympics – since). At Cambridge he met Chris Chataway and Roger Bannister, and together they became the team which plotted to get Bannister to the first-ever sub-four minute mile, achieved eventually on May 6th 1954. This was at a match between the AAA and Oxford University at the university's Iffley Road running track – in those days, of course, a cinder track, not tartan. (Incidentally, Bannister was also a climber: in his recent autobiography there is a photograph of him and Brasher climbing the Finsteraarhorn, the highest peak in the Bernese Oberland.)

Unlike what happens nowadays on the international athletics circuit, in the 1950s pacemakers in races were not allowed; any race with an overt pacemaker who would drop out after two or three laps would have the results nullified by the AAA, and subsequently by the IAAF. So the three had to be very careful to avoid behaving on the track as though outright pacemaking was going on. Brasher led the race for the first two laps, Chataway took on the lead for the third lap, and finally Bannister took over for the last lap and ran himself into the history books. The other two had to finish the race, of course, to avoid a pacemaking charge; but really, few people were interested in anything else about the match other than the world- record-breaking result of the mile.

Later that year Bannister also won the mile at the Empire and Commonwealth Games in Edmonton, beating the Australian John Landy, who had by then deprived him of the mile record. Yet, astonishingly, in December the inaugural BBC Sports Personality of the Year was won by Chataway, not Bannister, essentially because of setting a new world record for the 5000 metres and in so doing beating the Soviet hard man Vladimir Kuts.

Brasher, though, achieved further honours, and in some respects the biggest prize of all: he won the 3000 metre steeplechase in the Melbourne Olympic Games in 1956, confirmed after an initial protest had looked as though he might have been disqualified for interference. Subsequently, he brought the sport of orienteering to Britain, in 1957. He became a sports journalist, working his way up to become a star columnist for The Observer, though newspapers weren't his only arrow. He was for a time head of the Outside Broadcast unit of the BBC (at least, I *think* he held that position; the most I could find nowadays was that he was the *presenter* of the following programme), and in that capacity he is probably best remembered for masterminding the televised broadcast of the ascent of the Old Man of Hoy, a 450 feet high sandstone sea-stack off the island of Hoy in the Orkneys, in the summer of 1967, which pulled in the cream of British rock-climbing to an extravaganza spread out over two days.

Back in the 1950s the Pen y Gwryd hotel in North Wales had become the spiritual home of the Everest team in the months leading up to their departure for Nepal. There are still signatures of some members of the expedition on the ceiling in the bar, and it is regarded very much as a climbers' pub. It is situated at a junction on the road between Capel Curig and Beddgelert. Almost all the buildings here are connected with the pub, but on the other side of the road there used to be a garage. There are still bits of an unsightly concrete infrastructure on view, though how long it is since it functioned as a garage is anyone's guess – it's over 50 years since I first visited the area, and it was closed then. But the land must have belonged to someone, because in the 1970s (1980s?) it was widely rumoured in the climbing world that Brasher had bought the land and gifted it to the National Trust, to help prevent its being used for any other purpose. Everyone I've ever talked to about this, including some who have lived in the area for decades, has heard the same rumour, but no one knows if it's true.

John Disley was born in the same year as Chris Brasher, 1928. He won the bronze medal in the steeplechase at the Helsinki Olympics of 1952, and in 1955 had the world's fastest time, though he was injured at the time the team was selected for the Melbourne Olympics the following year. Like Brasher, however, he was interested in climbing and mountaineering, and when in 1955 the Central Council for Physical Recreation (CCPR) bought the old Royal Hotel at Capel Curig in North Wales to use as a centre for outdoor activities, Disley was appointed as Chief Instructor; there is still a photograph of him in this capacity up in the Centre. And while there, he wrote an instructional book, "Tackle Climbing This Way". A more retiring person than Brasher, he nonetheless had a public face through being appointed as a vice-chairman of the Great Britain Sports Council, a position he held from 1974 to 1982. Together, Brasher and Disley were to have a powerful influence over the way that mass fun-running was to develop in Britain during the 1980s.

The People's Marathon

The canoe trip described earlier, in the summer of 1980, was getting ahead of things. In November 1979, in his capacity as a star columnist for The Observer newspaper, Chris Brasher wrote the following:

"Last Sunday, in one of the most violent, trouble-stricken cities in the world, 11,532 men, women and children from 40 countries of the world, assisted by 2.5 million black, white and yellow people, Protestants and Catholics, Jews and Muslims, Buddhists and Confucians, laughed, cheered and suffered during the greatest public festival the world has ever seen."

He was, of course, writing about the New York marathon, and he clearly saw the prospect of something like this event being transplanted to London, engaging not just the runners but also the tens of thousands of residents living alongside wherever the route might eventually go. On the face of it this looked as though it would be an innovation, but even before it became reality he had been gazumped.

At the time, if you wanted to take part in an athletics event authorised by the AAA you were supposed to be affiliated to them. Normally this would be by being a member of an athletics club – Birchfield Harriers, or Coventry Godiva Harriers, and so on. Recognising that not everyone wanted to join a club, the AAA had a rule stipulating that an unattached runner could run in AAA-accredited events, but only for a year. Any longer than that, and you had to join an affiliated organisation. However, they came to realise that this rule was unenforceable, and so proposed instead that there be a levy of 50p on all unattached runners for all events. (The 50p suggestion was a minimum; when, subsequently, London got going, they decided to institute a £1 charge.) But, as "Running" magazine pointed out, this system was open to abuse, and was in effect also unenforceable, as long as there wasn't a central register of club members – which there wasn't.

These considerations began to cause difficulties as soon as there were events organised for Joe (and Josephine) Public to take part in. Quite how he came to realise that there was a latent demand for such an event I don't know, but a man in the West Midlands, John Walker, decided in the late 1970s to organise a marathon which anyone could take part in, club member or not. This was before Brasher's article in "The Observer". It's quite difficult now finding out anything about what was called the People's Marathon, despite the fact that there were at least four such events with several thousand entrants each time. But as well as going to the USA to consult with the organisers of the New York and Boston marathons, Brasher and Disley came to Birmingham to talk to John Walker about staging an event such as they hoped to put on in the rather different environment of Britain.

I have the race programme for the third People's Marathon, in 1982, in front of me. It was sponsored mainly by Nike and the Birmingham Evening Mail, but there is no mention of the AAA anywhere in the document. This suggests to me that the two earlier races had no formal recognition or accreditation by the AAA, but that the same two sponsors had supported the two earlier events. Living in Birmingham I remember being vaguely aware of some publicity about a marathon which was to take place in the spring of 1980. This was to be independent of the AAA – that is, you didn't have to be a member of a club to take part. Probably, at the time, I thought wistfully about how good it would be to take part, but my shoulder was still in a dodgy state, and the later canoe holiday did nothing to show that the shoulder was in a fit state for serious pushing: the canoeing movement, pulling backwards on a paddle, is precisely opposite to that of propelling a wheelchair, where you push forwards. So, with respect to the first People's Marathon, I did absolutely nothing. Nor, to my shame, did I take any notice as it was reported locally, either in advance or afterwards in the results.

Things were about to change, however, because on a visit to my GP I must have grumbled about the state of my shoulder "two years after the initial injury …" and so on (any athlete who has had a chronic injury will relate to the experience). She said that the practice had just taken on a new physiotherapist, she was very good, and she was sure that if anyone could do something, Jill would be able to. Sceptical after two years of going nowhere, but happy to clutch at a straw (or so it seemed), I agreed to give it a go. The GP was right: Jill *was* good. She put in weeks of heavy electrical work on the shoulder, as well as some deep frictions, which broke down the adhesions which had been troubling me for so long, and made it possible to go long-distance pushing again. The prospects for 1981 looked good.

The First Skirmish

The record of my early contacts with Brasher is incomplete. His 1979 article about the New York Marathon can still be found on the web, and it is an important landmark in charting the development of mass fun-running in this country. I don't seem to have replied to this, but 11 months later, in October 1980, I sent a letter to the Sports Editor, which reads as though it *was* a response to that article, to which Brasher himself replied the following month – see below for this correspondence. Why I should have replied to an article which had appeared 11 months earlier, without a further stimulus, is baffling; but there must have been something which provoked it, including (probably) some remark by Brasher about establishing a marathon in London the following year. (Even now, I think that is an incredibly short time to set up an event as complicated as a mass marathon.) Whatever the real situation regarding our correspondence, the main story began with my letter below:

"28th October 1980
The Sports Editor
The Observer
8 St Andrews Hill
London EC4

Dear Sir
Chris Brasher writes with eloquence and passion about the New York marathon, and why there needs to be a similar event held in London. The Observer, the GLC and Gillette are to be congratulated on their imagination, and one hopes the effort of organisation will be seen as worthwhile by all three. But there is one aspect of the affair of which even Chris Brasher may be unaware, and to which I should like to draw his and the organisers' attention.

He observed with amusement last year the waiter with the tray and the bottle of Perrier, and with great respect, the blind man who completed the course. He did not see, for they are now formally banned from entering the New York marathon, anyone pushing him (or her) self in a wheelchair. Had he visited, or run in, the Boston Marathon, or the Orange Bowl marathon, or any one of dozens of lesser-known events which occur the length and breadth of the USA, this sight would not have been denied him.

The conventional way in which wheelchair sports are reported in this country is not conducive to their being regarded very highly as sporting activities. It is the "human interest" approach which for some reason appeals to press and broadcasters alike, and which serves only to perpetuate the outdated image of people in wheelchairs as dependent, incapable, requiring sympathy, and so on. Most of the sports participated in by wheelchair athletes do not, I believe, have much spectator appeal, in that they seem mostly to show people in wheelchairs doing what people with legs that work also do, only not so well – ideal for the sympathy-evoking human interest story, but no use for anything else.

Wheelchair racing is sufficiently different from its able-bodied counterpart – running – to exist as a spectator sport in its own right, and the sight – which Chris Brasher has obviously <u>not</u> seen – of 20 people in wheelchairs lined up in front of the runners at the start of a major marathon is now commonplace in the USA. Although wheelchair participation in marathons is only just over five years old, times have been slashed to such an extent that the record is now one hour 55 minutes (some 13½ minutes faster than the fastest-ever runner, for what it is worth) set on the Boston course earlier this year. This is attributable to a mixture of improved wheelchair design and (particularly) to the fact that maintaining momentum in a wheelchair is quite different from (and easier than) doing so when running, even though it is the arms that do the propelling, not the legs.

Concern is sometimes expressed that wheelchair athletes are competing against runners. This is nonsense (that is, to be concerned about it is nonsensical): they take part <u>with</u> them, and there can be no better example of the fulfilment of the "Sport for All" slogan than this. Will the organisers and sponsors of the London marathon have the imagination to establish a wheelchair section for their new venture? I for one hope so, and I am sure they would find a response.

Yours sincerely

Tim Marshall (a wheelie)

PS It also needs a careful course design. Can I offer my services?"

(A brief comment: the organiser of the New York marathon, Fred le Bow, was already well known amongst wheelies in the USA for his opposition to wheelchair participation in "his" race. This antipathy reached such a pitch that in later years he was sued by wheelchair users for depriving them of their civil rights, through his use of public facilities – roads, pavements etc. – where the course was designed to exclude wheelchairs; there were kerbs and, I believe, on one occasion, a short flight of steps. I never heard the outcome of the case.)

"THE OBSERVER

1ˢᵗ November 1980

Dear Mr Marshall
Many thanks for your letter of October 26ᵗʰ – it has gone to the Letters Editor, but if he doesn't have space I will use extracts in my article this week.

I took special notice last Sunday of the Wheelies who finished (unofficially) in the New York Marathon and it would certainly be the management committee's wish that they could take part in the London Marathon, but we have got an awful lot of prejudice to overcome. To begin with it hasn't been easy to overcome the Police's reluctance and I am sure that in the first year we have got to accept some restrictions – notably those imposed by the athletic authorities who often have a very Victorian attitude.

When we have finished our detailed work on the route, perhaps I can write to you again and ask you to go over it in your chair and see what you think.
        Yours sincerely,
        CHRIS BRASHER"

This sounded very encouraging, and I looked forward eagerly to his next letter – which never came.

1981: The Lakes Project

The United Nations designated 1981 as the International Year of Disabled People. What to do? One answer: it looked as though the first London Marathon might include a wheelchair section, surely a fitting state-ment-cum-demonstration of the abilities of some kinds of disabled people. But what else – was there anything that *I* could do, not in terms of fundrais-ing – I'd always been hopeless at that – but something that would mark the year as something special for me?

The answer came when friends in the climbing club invited me to spend New Year with them at the hut of one of their other climbing clubs in Patterdale. The switch was thrown on realising that, thanks to Jill, not only would I be able to do the Derwentwater circuit in April, but that there were other large lakes in the Lake District that you could push round on roads: specif-ically, Thirlmere, Coniston, Bassenthwaite, and the grand-daddy of them all, Windermere. Ullswater wasn't on, because there was no road between Howtown, on the eastern shore of the lake, and Glenridding, at the very south-western corner. So Ullswater was parked for the time being.

Sarah, daughter of the aforementioned friends, volunteered to come round Thirlmere with me. We set off on New Year's morning from the north-east corner going south along the east side of the lake on the A591, rationalising to ourselves that there would be less traffic that day than on any other. That may indeed have been the case, but there was still too much for comfort, and it was with some relief that we reached the end of the lake and were able to turn onto the service road built along the west side. The first stretch hadn't been very hilly, just a bit of up and down near the start, but the back road was a joy, flat as a pancake and no traffic at all. Sadly, I didn't record how long we took.

Another climbing club weekend came in early February, and this time Joan volunteered to come round Coniston with me, not walking all the way as Sarah had done but driving round and stopping at a convenient spot every two or three miles for refuelling (me). Again, I went clockwise, starting and finishing in the village. The main feature of the circuit was the steep climb shortly after the start, in effect a climb up to Brantwood, John Ruskin's house, and now a place to be visited – but not on this occasion. It was so steep that at one stage I wondered whether I would be able to make it without assistance, which, had it been necessary, would have left me distraught with a collapsed project, but fortunately I made it OK. (I should add that so far all these circuits were made using my ordinary, everyday, wheelchair.)

Bassenthwaite was scheduled for early March, but other things happened first. Mitch, the retired headmaster, rang me up. John Walker, of the People's Marathon, had been in touch. The governors of the race wanted to mark the UN Year of Disabled People by designating BSAD as one of the race charities; and did he think it might be possible to stage, say, a demonstration race by wheelchairs of, say, 5, or perhaps even 10, kilometres as a kind of curtain-raiser to the marathon? And so I came to speak with John Walker. He was slightly surprised when I suggested a full marathon – I thought I could get half a dozen local people to take part – but was quite happy when I reassured him that it wouldn't be a cowboy affair, but a serious athletic event. I cited recent American times to him – 2h 9m 1s in the Orange Bowl marathon at Miami, and 1h 55m at Boston, both from1980. Like most people at this time he hadn't realised how far the Americans (and Canadians) had taken the event; and whilst I said that we couldn't approach these times, we'd put on a reasonable show. All I had to do now was to find the participants. Mark agreed to try again, as did a couple of others whom I'd met through basketball, and a couple more joined in through the grapevine, one of whom was being pushed.

Bassenthwaite came first, however. A weekend based at the university's outdoor centre by the side of Coniston was the setting, and this time Dee, one of my post-graduate students, who was at the weekend with her husband, agreed to do the necessary stewarding. This was on the same basis as the Coniston affair: drive 3 miles or so to a refuelling stop, wait till I appeared, refuel, and on we go. Bassenthwaite was the least enjoyable of all the lakes: the A591 north of Keswick, which went along the east side of the lake, was narrow and twisty, often with high banks alongside the road preventing my seeing what was round the next corner – or, more to the point, preventing me being seen from behind. And when that stretch was over and we crossed to the west side to come back, I was on the A66, the main east–west road through the heart of the north Lakes to the west coast. The only saving grace was that this section of the route was built on top of the old Penrith–Keswick–Cockermouth railway line, and so was as flat as a pancake. As with the other two lakes I failed to record the time, but it was something under four hours. And I noticed that Bassenthwaite was the only lake done anti-clockwise – the first two had been clockwise, and the two to come would be also.

Having sat and waited for months for any further news from Chris Brasher about wheelchairs, I learned somehow – let's call it the grapevine – that wheelchairs wouldn't be included. As soon as this was confirmed, I wrote to him on March 23rd:

> "Dear Chris Brasher
> I'm sorry you weren't able to let me know whether wheelchairs were to be allowed in the London Marathon, though I heard on the grapevine that they were not. May I dare to hope that the franchise will be widened next year?
>
> Can I also let you know that London's loss is Chelmsley Wood's gain, for there will be half- a-dozen wheelchairs in the People's Marathon on May 10th this year.
>
> Best wishes for Sunday – I hope it is the success the project deserves.
>   Yours sincerely
>   Tim Marshall"

I never had a reply

***

Before May 10th, however, I was back to the Lakes Project. April was Derwentwater, and at last I was going to be able to take part. It was a particularly busy weekend, for Douglas Hurndall wanted me to help launch the Challenger Trimaran project at the Queen Mary reservoir at Datchet on the Saturday; Derwentwater was on the Sunday. Douglas picked me up at Reading station on the Friday evening, put me up at his home, and then on the Saturday morning we went to Datchet. Unfortunately, the weather was awful: not raining, but blowing a hooley, Force 8, and it was thought to be unwise to let a total novice out on the water, a sentiment I could only agree with. So the designer, Rod McAlpine-Downie, took the boat out for a few reaches under the eyes of a few cameras – the yachting press had been well primed – and then we all went home; or in my case on a train up to Lancaster – guard's van of course, along with a pile of people looking after their bicycles – and changing for Barrow where I was to stay with Colin, another climbing club member, the husband of Joan and, more to the point, a fell-runner who was going to run round Derwentwater with me. The gales down south had been matched by heavy weather up north; specifically, a 6" blanket of snow on the Thursday evening. At the time, I didn't think this would really matter because it disappeared over Friday night and Saturday morning almost as quickly as it had arrived.

At the school in Keswick on the Sunday morning – the school had become, *de facto*, the headquarters of the whole operation – there was a full complement of pupils, staff, police and local volunteers; and almost no participants. The snow which had arrived overnight on Thursday had provoked a torrent of cancellations on the Friday, too late, however, to cancel the food, which on the Sunday morning lay on trestle tables in the school entrance hall demurely wrapped in cellophane, enough for 60 people. Bill Parkinson had handed on the local organisation to someone else from the north-east, but his own cancellation came along with all the others on the Friday. Too bad that by Sunday morning the only remaining snow was on sheltered, north-facing slopes, or on the very tops. In the end there were only nine participants. I started off hoping to get somewhere near Gerry Kinsella's 1h 28m, but 2½ years of relative inactivity meant I wasn't nearly fit enough, and I only managed 1h 55m. It may have been the problem with the food which led to the following year's being the last-ever such event; it had run its course, been fantastic while it lasted, but now was the time to close it. I never discovered what happened to all the food.

The four lakes I'd been round so far had all been done using my everyday chair, an Everest and Jennings, which weighed about 40 lbs. Good of its kind at the time, it was definitely not a racing chair, but the lake circuits were not races, rather me just bumbling round. The marathon would, I supposed, be different. From somewhere I heard that there were two Dutch racing chairs, Hofmeisters, acquired by the local Lions club using funds raised by the first of the "Sutton Park Brands Hatch" events. They were kept at Wyndley Leisure Centre, but sort of belonged to the Wilson Stuart special school, which was willing for others to use them provided their own children didn't need them at the time. Since the kids only needed them during the week, the headmaster, Colin Grantham, was happy for me to use one at the weekend, and happier still when I offered to pay him £5 each time I did so.

The Hofmeister chairs were intended to be a club chair, and were thus widely adjustable. Seat and back-rest up and down, footplates of course, axle position up and down and fore and aft, large wheels (the same size, 26", that I'd seen on the Australian chairs at Stoke Mandeville three years earlier), and small handrims which gave a gearing effect when pushing on the flat or downhill, but made it much harder pushing uphill (even then, international regulations had got as far as proscribing more than one handrim per wheel, so you couldn't have a suite of rims to suit all gradients). The bearings were much better than those of my chair, so it would go faster, but it was made of steel and with all the facilities for adjusting everything under the sun, it was even heavier than mine. I hoped the drag of the extra weight would be outdone by the extra speed (in the event, it was).

This is the article I wrote for John Walker about the race, which appeared in the race programme the following year. With a small amount of editing (not by me!) it also appeared in "Running" magazine:

"The London Marathon didn't want to know, so John Walker's enlightened attempt to stage the first wheelchair marathon in this country to be integrated with runners came to fruition. There are six of us at the start, one being pushed and five self-propelled; we start before everyone else, of course, to avoid notching dozens of Achilles tendons as victims of the footplates. By the time the runners catch us up, both we and they will be well spaced out and any danger to them will be over.

The gun goes at last. It's a downhill start and very soon Mark and I, in the only two proper racing chairs (both borrowed) leave the others for dead. It's fast, faster than I've been before in a chair, but in this weather you need windscreen wipers for your eyes. We slow down as the horrible truth of the first hill looms. Horrible, because I soon realise that I've put too small handrims on the chair, too small to give adequate leverage to power up hills, and already Mark is hanging around waiting for me. I tell him to get on and forget about our finishing together; thereafter I only see him coming back along opposite sides of dual carriageways.

The motorway section [*NB this was before the M42 opened to traffic; part of it was used in the marathon*] is only fractionally downhill, but what a beautiful ride – it has stopped drizzling, too, and before the runners have caught up I sweep past the first feeding station, arm out to grab a sponge. And there goes Mark, back up the other side – wonder how far to the turn. The slight downhill becomes a laborious uphill, but the runners begin to flock past and there is an almost continuous stream of encouragement. "Well done, lad." "You're bloody marvellous." "Can I have a lift?"

Another long dual carriageway – Mark again – and then a very unsettling, bumpy, narrow, twisty footpath, too much height lost too quickly, and – Christ, a kerb! Two people obviously detailed to lift the chair over, and then try to get a rhythm back. My fingers hurt like hell – I have gloves, but I didn't tape the fingers individually, and I already have blisters, less than half-way round. Stop at a St John's post for taping. Ray, whom I knew at school and who had appeared just before the start, runs past. "You've cracked, Marshall, you've cracked." A short steep climb out of an underpass and a girl comes out of the crowd and starts pushing me. She seems offended to be asked to stop. Too bad. Back onto a road, and here beginneth the second circuit. Hope I can get round – probably all depends on the fingers. More drizzle, more hills – the later memories are nearly all of up rather than down – but at three months distance the memories even of the first are telescoped!

Except the finish. Along the road, roaring crowds, and – help – a steep grass bank covered in matting, liberally smeared in mud. I start at it but get nowhere. I try diagonally for a zig-zag, but a runner comes along and shoves me five yards up the very steep bit. Hmm, does the whole thing still count or not? Still grass – can't get the leverage on the handrims, and have to push the wheels – very slow. The small front wheels reach the tarmac and as the chair begins to freewheel a bit there's a roar from all around – somehow they realise how different from tarmac – and difficult – grass is. A large digital clock looms (4 hours 9 minutes – plus 17, of course, disappointingly slow); as I reach it someone pours champagne (sparkling wine?) over me and throws three Mars bars onto my lap.

The others are all looking relaxed at the finish, with half-marathons under their wheels. All but Mark, who's in the first aid tent after throwing up. Does he realise he holds the British Wheelchair Marathon record? Who the hell wants a Mars bar? I want to live in a warm bath for a week. Wonder if, after this, the London lot will let us in next year?"

(Jim also finished the race, in 4h 50m.)

It was a start, though without the immediate consequences we all wished for. But with London in particular, and of course its television transmission, the whole country seemed to go wild with staging marathons (not, in the first instance, half-marathons or 10k races). It was as though every local authority needed to stage a race (always "The FIRST Somewhere Marathon", thus implying there was to be a dynasty – which, of course, in many cases there wasn't), demonstrating their importance to the local population and, almost, the justification for the existence of their Leisure and Recreation departments, which, with the exception of libraries, were a non-statutory element of local authority responsibilities, and just beginning to come under increasing financial pressure near the start of the first Thatcher government.

A couple of weeks later Mark came back from a weekend at Stoke Mandeville – he'd been there for a training session with the Paraplegic Athletic Association. Track work had never interested me, so I didn't go to that sort of thing. But he brought news of a forthcoming wheelchair road race, "just for wheelchairs" I understood him to say, at Newcastle, a half- marathon. After the experience of the People's Marathon I was sceptical about a wheelchair only race, and said so; but he persuaded me to apply. He'd brought an entry form, but the closing date had already gone, so I sent off the form with a covering letter outlining what I'd done in helping to organise the Derwentwater affair, the Sutton Park races and, most recently, in taking part in the People's Marathon. Almost by return of post I had a letter telling me I'd been accepted into the first-ever running of the Great North Run (what a brilliant title, I thought).

A couple of weeks before the event I had a letter outlining the arrangements for the start. Alarm bells rang, because although the organisers had announced prizes for the first three wheelchairs, they had also said that we should join the athletes at the start in accordance with our estimated finishing times, guidance for which would be provided in the form of large banners by the side of the start showing estimated finishing times every 15 minutes. As a recipe for a disaster for wheelchair racing, and for the runners starting in front of us, this could hardly have been bettered. I wrote immediately, explaining the American practice of giving the wheelchairs a short headstart, which also enabled the wheelchair section to be identified as a distinct race within the overall occasion, and provided the maximum safety for both wheelchair users and, particularly, runners. Within a very short time I had another letter, which had obviously been sent to all the self-propelled wheelchairs, advising us that the starting arrangements had been changed, and that the self-propelled wheelchairs would now all start in front, with a headstart of 5 minutes.

There were about 20 of us milling about at the start, some of whom I recognised as being from the hospital sports club, and some from the basketball circuit. Amongst all, however, there was the same topic of conversation: "Did you apply to London?" "Did you get in?" "Did you tell them you were in a chair?" "What did they say?" "What are you going to do next year?" "What's Stoke doing?" In this context "Stoke" meant Stoke Mandeville, which at the time was only concerned with people with spinal injury, and here, there were evidently some amputee, non-spinal injury wheelchair people about to take part. And, as far as I knew, Stoke had nothing to do with organising road racing. I learned later that the wheelchair element of the race had been proposed by, and argued for, by Carole Bradley, who had an important role in working for BSAD in the North-East, across all disabilities. I never found out what the distinct areas of responsibility of Carole and Bill Parkinson were.

And so, off we went. If the start of the People's Marathon was faster than I'd ever been in a chair before, this was like going down a bobsleigh run (but without the sharp corners). It was dry, which was definitely a tick in the "go faster" column. But more than that, it began with a mile and a half descent down the motorway which went north to south through the middle of the city. At that stage, no one wore a helmet, and to my embarrassment I found myself braking for parts of the descent, simply because I was scared by how fast I was going. The course flattened out on reaching the New Tyne Bridge (the one that looks like a mini- Sydney Harbour bridge) and climbed up to pass through Gateshead. The race gave rise to one of the great early pictures of wheelchair road racing in this country, with Mick Kelly, a single leg amputee from Sheffield, being snapped on the Tyne bridge shoulder-to-shoulder with Mike McLeod, one of the top road-runners of the day. Of course they weren't in direct competition, but as an exhibition of one type of integration it could hardly be bettered.

Still trying to work out the best combination of seat height, seat angle, pushing rim diameter, gloves and so on, on this occasion I got the gloves wrong, and ended up fourth, the race being won by Alan Robinson from Doncaster, whom I knew through the basketball team. But what made it stand apart from the People's Marathon was the crowds – the crowds of spectators. The route was almost all on dual carriageway, with both sides seemingly crammed several people deep all the way along (the weather was better too, which no doubt helped). Apart from the start, the main feature of the course I remember was Marsden Hill: about 1½ miles from the finish, there was a steep downhill of 100 yards at about 1 in 8 (maybe even 1 in 6), followed immediately by a sharp left turn and a gentle undulating mile-and-a-bit to the finish. And, as far as I could tell, and apart from the initial hiccup, there had been no quibbling about the wheelchairs starting in front, and so constituting a separate race within the overall event. Look at this, London.

Another Interlude

A friend of mine from work was a statistician in the academic department of Physical Education. As one of his duties he had taken over running the British end of an exchange with PE students from Charles University in Prague. The nature of this exchange was that the British students went over to Prague in early January, and then to a mountain hut in the Krkonoše mountains on the Czech–Polish border, to be introduced to skiing, both downhill and cross-country, whilst the Czech students came over to England in July to be introduced to sailing, rock-climbing and orienteering (most of them had already a lot of experience of kayaking), based on the university's outdoor centre near Coniston. They then spent a couple of days in Birmingham, and a few more in London, before returning home.

The Iron Curtain was still in place, and exchanges like this were one of few ways that the Czech students could experience the West. There was, so we understood, considerable competition to get on this exchange, which always had two members of staff from the department at Charles University, at least one of whom was a fully badged-up member of the Party to keep an eye on, and no doubt report on, any students showing overt signs of dissent. Mostly, there was very little trouble of any kind, though the male Czech students found it rather demeaning to be expected to take a full part in running the centre, doing what they regarded as women's work: preparing the food, including cooking, laying the tables, washing-up and cleaning, including the toilets.

I had no instructional qualifications in anything, and many of the activities – hill-walking, rock-climbing, abseiling (Hodge Close quarry), white-water canoeing – were in effect out of bounds to me. But I could, and did, take people sailing, in GP 14s, where I sat transversely across the stern of the boat and issued instructions to one, or occasionally two, people up front regarding moving from side to side of the boat, pulling or slackening the jib-sheet, and so on. Over the years, the most challenging of these trips was taking one of the Czech staff members, who had never sailed before, and spoke no English, down the lake from the Centre at Torver to Peel Island, lunching there, and returning safely. The conversation was in French, which we both had, to an adequate extent at least. There was no point in using sailing jargon when telling him what to do – I didn't know the correct jargon anyway – so "tighten the jib-sheet" became "tirez la corde", with other instructions similarly turned into the vernacular.

Windermere

Although the main purpose of my going to Coniston was to help with, and indeed be part of, the Czech exchange, with another member of the climbing club, Steve Oliphant (a fell-runner), I had planned to finish off the big five lakes by doing Windermere. So, on the Tuesday evening after the meal, clearing away and a wash, I took off and parked overnight in a lay-by near Ambleside on the road from Coniston, meeting Stephen and his wife, Wendy, in the Waterside car park at the northern end of Windermere at 5.50 on the Wednesday morning. And I used the Hofmeister chair – it would be a lot quicker than mine.

There were no time constraints, this wasn't a race, but the complete circuit, at over 28 miles, was about twice the length of the previously-longest lake, Bassenthwaite. We didn't want to be caught in the middle of heavy tourist traffic, and it was the middle of the tourist season, so it was imperative to get the busiest part of the route out of the way as soon as possible. Hence we went clockwise, down the A591 to Windermere, or at least to the junction with the road coming down from the Kirkstone Pass (itself done from the other side over 20 years later), where we turned onto the A592 to Bowness and, more or less hugging the shore, on to the bottom end of the lake at Newby Bridge. We left at exactly 6 o'clock, and Wendy played the same role as had Dee, my post-graduate student, in going round Bassenthwaite: she drove the car, and every five miles or so stopped in a convenient lay-bay to feed us nuts, raisins, dates and drink. Stupidly (again), I didn't record intermediate times.

The first half of the circuit was on bigger roads with better surfaces than the return half up the west side, and was correspondingly quicker. The return offered several options between Graythwaite Hall and Hawkshead. The one I think I took held to the left at the Hall, then three kilometres further north kept to the left again at Eel House, bringing me along the west side of Esthwaite Water and so up to Hawkshead, where all the possible routes merged.

By Hawkshead I remember feeling a bit tired, with what I had anticipated to be the steepest part yet to come: the climb off the minor roads I'd been on ever since Newby Bridge, and on to the main A-road between Coniston and Ambleside at Clappersgate. With more than a marathon already gone, I *was* tired, but there was only 1½ miles to go. I had to zig-zag to get up the hill (an uphill slalom – interesting) – and Stephen was quite busy over this stretch and on into Ambleside, fending off traffic which by now was quite as busy as we had anticipated. But we pulled into the Waterside car park at 4 minutes to 12; 5 hours 56 minutes. Wendy had managed to find a parking space despite all the tourist traffic. Was this a good time? Who knew? How could you tell? Eight hours would have felt – and would have been – inordinately long, whilst four hours would have been implausibly short; so there weren't really any meaningful comparisons to be made.

Except that – I had in mind a report in "Sports 'n Spokes" from a year or two back about two wheelchair users who had pushed round the Great Salt Lake in Utah. (Actually, it might not have been the whole way round, because the complete circuit is about 180 miles.) I remembered the distance as 116 miles, which might be incorrect but it was certainly in three figures. And their time was in the upper teens of hours. It rather put Windermere into the shade.

And then Stephen, seeking for further excursions to do, suggested the long trip – John o' Groats to Land's End. At this stage I hadn't heard of anyone who had done this, and not even the grapevine revealed anything. In any case it would need a longer stretch of time than I usually had for holidays, and that might be tricky to negotiate. It was something to think about, anyway. Then came news of further heroics from across the pond (again reported in "Sports 'n Spokes"), because after the 1981 Boston Marathon, and in celebration of the United Nations having declared 1981 to be the International Year of Disabled People, two prominent American wheelchair athletes, George Murray and Phil Carpenter, challenged each other to do the American equivalent of our long trip, one which, however, was done rather less frequently than ours: Los Angeles to New York, finishing on the top floor of the UN building. This trans-America challenge got me thinking about a European equivalent, Istanbul to London or, more specifically, the Bosporus Bridge to Tower Bridge, an expedition which finally came to fruition in 1986. But that was five years away. Returning to local possibilities, Stephen said that, in spite of the lack of a road all the way round, he'd think further about Ullswater.

The marathon scene seemed to be calming down, with only a few left in places that held little attraction for me. Except that, at what seemed fairly short notice, Birmingham announced the City of Birmingham Marathon, to be held in early- to mid-September. Not one I could miss, really, and so I entered along with Mark (he'd had a very bad Great North Run) and a number of others who had been at the People's Marathon and other, shorter races from here and there.

It was a loop course, and the wheelchairs were allowed a headstart. Beginning at the National Exhibition Centre, it wound its way through the outer suburbs of the east side of the city, into the centre and along Colmore Row, and past the Council House and the Town Hall (half way, for those wishing to do only a half marathon). There, a commentator for the local radio seemed to be utterly astonished when a wheelchair hove into view, screaming with excitement and attempting a live interview as I pushed past him at a pace far faster than he could keep up; I wasn't going to slow down for him, or anyone else come to that. The route went out of the city on the Stratford road, winding through further outer suburbs before reaching the NEC again. The finish was inside one of the main exhibition halls, but there was a pavement which you had to be lifted onto. Fortunately, someone in the organisation was prepared for this, and there were three or four men ready to lift me up and over the kerb.

The time? 3h 37m 19s, almost 50 minutes faster than my People's Marathon time, one which at the time I thought was probably a British record, and said so to the interviewer at the finish. Curiously, they didn't seem particularly interested in the idea, so I let it drop. In any case, to put my time in an international context, in April the year before (1980) Boston had been done in 1h 55m, so it was all too obvious we were light years behind. Later, maybe even the following year, I heard that Gerry had done the Humber Bridge marathon in 3h 15m, the same day as the Birmingham race, or a week later, so I decided to have a go at that in 1982, always assuming the race would be run again that year.

As far as I was concerned that was it for the inaugural wheelchair road-racing season. No one had a complete overview of what races were being done by whom, when, and in what time; but whatever races I went to I asked the organisers to send me a list of the finishing times, and asked the racers themselves to let me know what they had done in events elsewhere. And always, there was the question "Are you going to (try to) enter London next year?"

There was, however, an important development regarding the general case for wheelchair racing as part of mass fun-running. In an article in "Sports 'n Spokes", the (American) National Wheelchair Athletic Association set out the case for why, and how, races should and could include wheelchair sections. All the elements which we had discovered by trial and error were set out with a clear explanation of what was needed (basically, a headstart, no kerbs or steps, and an open-minded attitude by the race organisers). The article was called "Sharing the Road" and was to prove useful in making the case in future for the inclusion of a wheelchair section in road races. I never thought to send it to "Running" magazine.

A Final Interlude

A few weeks after the Birmingham marathon there was an approach from Stoke about winter sports. There was a centre in Norway, Beitostolen, dedicated to developing and promoting winter sports for disabled people, and more was beginning to be reported from America in "Sports 'n Spokes". The American reports revolved around the use on snow of the pulk, the Norwegian sledge I had seen at the spinal unit in Denver three years earlier; and on developments in design (the Arroya) which provided a sharper edge to the runners underneath, giving greater control laterally when going downhill. It was not, however, a proper downhill piece of equipment, and couldn't be controlled the way skis could.

Stoke had sent a couple of people out to Norway to see what was going on, and they returned with information about the pulk and two other pieces of equipment for use on ice rinks: one, a sledge propelled by short sticks which was used for ice hockey, and the other, a different kind of sledge also propelled by sticks, but much longer and used for racing. There wasn't, isn't and I would guess never will be, a proper 400 metre ice-racing track in Britain, but the prospects for sledge ice-hockey were much brighter – after all, there are many ice-rinks in Britain, and many ice-hockey clubs, so the idea of the sport wasn't completely foreign.

Whatever the circulation list was, I was one of those invited to Solihull ice-rink one Saturday evening to be introduced to the sports and the equipment and, as far as possible, to try them out. Over the next few years I became involved with both hockey and racing, but for me the most important development was getting access, not to a pulk itself, but to the mould from which they were made. My climbing club friends had been talking about getting me out to the Alps at New Year on their skiing trip, though how they thought I might spend my time with no real means of propulsion for the wheelchair in, on or across snow I cannot now remember. But using a pulk – here was something that opened up new possibilities.

No one at Solihull wanted the mould, so I took it. A friend at work was into glass fibre, having just designed and built a racing dinghy, so making a pulk was as easy as a picnic in the park. So we did. And I took it to Switzerland in late December for a fortnight's holiday, the like of which I couldn't even have imagined a few months earlier. The next year, the original pulk being demonstrably a bit short for me, we built another, longer model, made a mould from the model, and then pressed out a new, longer pulk, which served for 25 years until late complications of my original injury put a stop to all the winter sporting activities. The original mould ended up in a special school on the east side of Birmingham under the guardianship of one of the city Outdoor Education advisors.

Next Steps

There was no central organisation or information point where people could find out what races had been done and with what times, what races had turned wheelchair applicants down, for those races which had accepted wheelchairs what the courses were like (flat or hilly, twisty or with long straights, open or closed roads and so on). But information percolated through in a rather patchwork manner, giving *some* information about *some* races which *might* be useful for the following year, if the race was going to be staged again (not all were). For example, Gerry Kinsella's 3h 15m on the Humber Bridge marathon, some time in late September, removed whatever pretensions I had to holding the fastest time in Britain; if asked, I said I held it for a week, though it could have been two weeks or not at all. And somehow, we needed wheelchair marathoning to be taken seriously, above the level of individual races accepting the odd wheelchair applicant. I had no idea how to set about doing this, but one or two things occurred, almost like drips on a stone which eventually wear a a hole, which slowly nudged things forward. And rather quicker than water on a stone.

In July 1981, Liz Dendy (from the Water Sports Division of the Sports Council) wrote to me:

> "Dear Tim, Kath Pollitt of our North West region approached me some time ago saying that the Manchester Marathon had refused to accept wheelchair applicants. I then wrote to the Secretary of the British Marathon Runners Club, asking them whether they had a policy on this. I enclose a copy of his reply, and I wondered whether you might feel like writing an article for their magazine. Please don't feel you have to!"

There ensued some correspondence with the secretary to the BMRC, Terry Lewins, about why and how wheelchair athletes could be included in "ordinary" marathons (or road races in general). He pointed out that the BMRC was more an information source than anything else, and suggested that I write to the AAA, who, as the governing body for athletics, could issue a policy statement about the inclusion of wheelchairs. My files failed to reveal any interaction with the AAA, though it's worth pointing out that they hadn't made a big noise about the Great North Run, which they had fully accredited, and with wheelchairs starting in front, too. This last point was still an issue two years later.

These exchanges led to other contacts, because late in 1981 "Running" magazine asked me to write an article about wheelchair marathoning (I don't have the original request, but do have the article I wrote and the acceptance letter by a sub-editor, Alison Turnbull, dated January 6th 1982). "Running" had exploded in popularity quite as much as the activity it reported on; that it had accepted the article could only do good for the cause, since I assumed the magazine would be read by any race organiser wanting to pick up tips, and generally to find out what was going on elsewhere; including, I supposed, Brasher and Disley.

Entering the 1982 London race was the next step. I don't remember the details of how you were supposed to do this, but clearly whatever method had been used in 1981 was deemed inadequate. I do remember that you had to queue at a main post office and hand your form in at some unearthly hour in the morning, so I set the alarm clock for a suitably early time. But then, on the local radio late in the evening, I heard that queues were already forming for the handing-in time several hours later. So, a quick wash, and into town clutching an entry form and, almost inevitably, bumping into both university staff and medical students bent on the same mission. And by the time that a special section of the office opened at (?) 6 in the morning, there were hundreds, if not thousands, of marathon hopefuls waiting to hand in the form. As with all AAA-accredited events, you had to sign at the end of the form to say that you would abide by AAA laws regarding the running of the race. I did sign it, but in the light of what could be described as the frosty reception by Chris Brasher to the prospect of a wheelchair section in his race, didn't state that I was a wheelchair user.

It was Liz Dendy who suggested that I write to John Disley about a wheel-chair section in London – but please to keep her name out of it, because he was Vice-Chairman of the Sports Council, whilst she was an employee; an entirely reasonable request, I thought. Curiously, amidst three inches thick correspondence about the race, this is one exchange that I don't have copies of; what happened to them, or why I didn't keep the letters, I don't know. But the gist of my letter to him will have been – the usual case: everyone else is doing it, the times, while slow by American standards, are respectable and can only improve, and it needs properly organising rather than coping with *ad hoc* participants as they turn up on the day. I can only imagine his reply, largely in the light of what ensued over the next 3–4 months, but it will have been very dismissive, and made clear that there was no place for wheelchairs, or a wheelchair section, in their foot-race. And that seemed to be that, as far as London and 1982 were concerned.

At this point I should introduce several others who came to have some part to play over the next 15 months and beyond. I cannot pinpoint the exact time that they emerged as part of the story, nor the precise event which propelled them on stage; but they all did play a role which was important at the time.

I first saw Philip Lewis on my first visit the "The Nationals" in 1973. He was a tetraplegic (a broken neck), but a formidable table-tennis player, and also a qualified solicitor. I met him on and off during 1981 at various conferences and workshops being staged as part of the Year of Disabled People. Of greater relevance is that he was a member of the Sports Council, having assumed the (formally unstated) role of disabled champion from Norman Croucher, and in this capacity he will have been well-known to John Disley. He was also quite high up in the hierarchy of BSAD, though I wasn't aware of that, having little to do with the organisation *per se*. By the time of the 1983 race he had become Chairman.

Mike O'Flynn retired from a senior officer post in the army in his 50s, and like many in a similar position looked around for something else to do (Douglas Hurndall at the RYA Seamanship Foundation, the sponsor of the Challenger trimaran, took a similar route). I don't know, and it's not relevant, which regiment Mike came from, but at some time in the early 1980s he was appointed as CEO of BSAD. Near the middle of the year, shortly after he had come across some of the waves I was creating, he bestowed on me the label "National Wheelchair Marathon Co-ordinator" and sent me some BSAD headed notepaper with the subtitle below it; it was a simple matter to produce more by photocopying as necessary.

BSAD had a patchwork of officers round the regions, which I never really understood. The West Midlands, for example, seemed to be run entirely by volunteers, with no paid staff at all. In the North-East, Carol Bradley was the queen bee, but whether she was a volunteer or a paid officer I never knew (by now, Bill Parkinson seemed to have disappeared off the scene altogether). And in London, +/- the South-East, Jenny Ward had a role in sports development for Disability Sport that I think was a paid job.

I didn't get a place in London, so the next thing to do was start entering other races. The "First Norfolk Marathon" sounded promising, to the uninitiated Norfolk being a flat county. It was, really. Norfolk was a point-to-point event, finishing in Norwich city centre but starting very near to the north coast, at a place called Holt. The organisers laid on buses to carry the runners from the town centre to the start; no special arrangements for the wheelies, so we had to bum our way up the steps and onto a seat. I say "we": this was the first time I came across Denise Smith, who for many years flew the flag for women's wheelchair road-racing in Britain.

I don't remember the start – how long a headstart we were given, if any – but the race itself was cursed by the weather, a south-westerly gale that blew strongly as we made our way south, along with cold flurries of rain; very cold flurries. I remember being surprised at the number of runners stopped by the side of the road waiting to be picked up – surely, if I could finish the thing, arm-powered, couldn't they, leg-powered? After the dreadful race conditions, surpassed for me only by the Humber Bridge race in the autumn, the finish was, for quite different reasons, equally memorable. You went through the finish line and were then shepherded round to the left and – into the cathedral. Here was the aftercare: hot drinks, massage stations, blankets and so on. And all overseen by His Grace the Bishop, who wandered around helping where he could, giving encouraging words when that was all he could do, and so on. As an example of the church temporal, it was supreme.

One other matter I particularly remember was the local media reception. A photo and short report eventually appeared in the local paper, but at the finish was a reporter from the local radio station. The race was, I think, the week before London, so when I was asked about the course, the race and so on, I praised the course but cursed the weather, and made sure to point out that if London had been as enlightened as they were in Norfolk, I wouldn't actually have been there at all; but that since London was blinkered, I was happy to come and do their race.

The First Battle Of Marathon

The May edition of "Running" magazine was published in late April. It included a short article by me, explaining how wheelchair road racing started, the best way of including a wheelchair section in a running race, what had been done so far in Britain, especially in contrast with the times being recorded in America (1h 48m 06 s in the 1982 Boston Marathon) and expressing frustration at the continued ban by London on wheelchairs. The magazine then went off to John Disley to seek his views on the matter. What follows is a direct quote of his response to the magazine:

> "The Gillette London Marathon is a 'foot-race' held under IAAF, AAA and WCCA Laws and Rules of Competition. It is not a multi-purpose jamboree [*really?*]. Any disabled person is entitled to apply for entry as long as they intend to traverse the course on foot.
>
> The wheelchair racers do, of course, deserve to have their sport developed and if it were possible to incorporate them into the London Marathon without threatening the efficiency, fairness and success of our running event no doubt their inclusion would be considered.
>
> The fact is we are straining our persuasive powers to the limit to achieve the route and timing we now have for 1982, and the inclusion of a wheelchair event in conjunction with our foot-race could only be done by eroding the quality of the race. This we are not prepared to do.
>
> In a few years time, things may change, but in the meantime the London Marathon will benefit charities to the extent of some £2 million-plus generated by the sponsorship of many of our runners."

I was appalled at reading this, and said so to the editorial assistant from "Running" who had sent me the magazine. As an afterthought, I added a PS at the end:

"Do you remember the time when women runners were forcibly pulled out of the Boston Marathon? Disley is inviting the same development with respect to wheelchair athletes."

I wasn't prepared to leave it at that, though, and wrote a vicious piece about a fictional interview with a former athlete, John Wiseley:

"What's it like if, as an active sportsman of international repute, you find yourself struck down by accident or disease? What sort of hopes do you have for the future? We went to interview John Wiseley, former international athlete and member of the Sports Council, who was severely injured in a car accident some months ago, leaving him paralysed from the waist down. Sitting in his wheelchair, he outlined to us how he plans to develop his life again.

"I know that my running days are over," he told us, "but there is the possibility of taking part in some wheelchair sports. Of course, now I am in a chair I realise that I am not a proper person any more, still less a real athlete. It means, for example, that I won't be able to take part in serious events like the London Marathon. There are many difficulties, you see: I can't carry a tray with a bottle of Perrier water on it, and the balloons and streamers which some athletes wear would get in the way of the wheelchair. Without these decorations, of course, wheelchairs taking part would make the whole thing look like a multi-purpose jamboree, and I wouldn't want that."

"Other things make it difficult as well," he went on. "I'm concerned with the quality of the event. After all, in the USA the best wheelchair times for the marathon are only around two hours, and this really isn't good enough for an important event like the London Marathon.

"The problem began, I think, when they first let women take part. They're so much slower than men, which means that the whole thing takes so much longer. I really think the organisers will have to think again about letting them take part. And as for letting wheelchairs in, with their times, they would

78

simply erode the quality of the race even more, and the organisers quite rightly shouldn't consider that.

"Of course, it is nice to know that the organisers want everyone to raise money for you, even if we're not allowed to do it ourselves. Real people don't have such a good opportunity to be patronised by such important people."

John Wiseley concluded his penetrating analysis with the following thoughts: "Even if I won't be able to enter the London race, there are other, less serious events in the provinces which are only too pleased to accept we poor cripples: Newcastle, Manchester [I'd entered the forthcoming Piccadilly Marathon, told them I was in a wheelchair, but hadn't been rejected], Hull, Birmingham, Norwich, Guilford and Cardiff, for example, where they obviously have a different view of handicapped people like us."

We left this humble, thoughtful man and returned to the city where 18,000 real athletes will soon be endeavouring to raise the standard of the London even higher than before."

I don't know if I sent this anywhere, or simply kept it, having vented my spleen at what I regarded as an ignorant and patronising view of things: "Not a multi-purpose jamboree" – what did he think of all the runners dressed up in fancy pantomime gear? "Eroding the quality of the race" – what did he think of the fastest wheelchair times in Britain, now rapidly approaching the 3-hour barrier with the prospect of getting down to the American times of 2 hours and below? I had concluded my reply to "Running" magazine by saying that I'd had my opportunity to make the case, and perhaps it was now time to let others take up the running. Then the PS thought came; and then there was the 1982 race, held on May 9th.

I didn't watch it, but listened to the radio commentary, fronted by Cliff Morgan. He was as enthusiastic as ever, obviously about the great effort the runners were putting in, but also about the huge crowd of spectators at the finish, mentioning in particular Margaret Maugham "...sitting in her wheelchair, the winner of the first gold medal for Britain in the first-ever Paralympic Games back in 1960 in Rome."

I didn't need any further invitation, writing to him the next day suggesting that as well as being spectators, some wheelchair users were actually pushing marathons themselves, and wouldn't it be a good idea if there was a wheelchair section in London? He replied, very quickly, on BBC notepaper on May 11th – the same day, that is, that he will have received my letter:

"Dear Mr. Marshall,
Thank you for your letter of 10th May. Certainly, I will speak with Chris and John Disley about the entries of people in wheelchairs for the London Marathon. I do not know what the situation is but I will enquire and let you know.

My very best wishes
        Yours sincerely
        Cliff Morgan
        Head of Outside Broadcasts Group, Television"

Rather irritatingly (and carelessly), I don't have copies of my letters to him, though I do remember writing back saying that making a case for a wheelchair section with B&D would get nowhere, because they were against, full stop. To his credit, he did reply, on June 1st:

"Dear Mr Marshall
Further to my last letter of 11th May, I now have some more information which I hope will help.

The reason why wheelchairs are difficult in the London Marathon is because there are so many tight bends and cobbled sections in the narrower streets of London which does make it a hazardous proposition for everyone concerned.

New York, of course, has lots of long straight runs which makes it a lot easier but then they have to restrict the number of wheelchairs very severely. [*This wasn't correct, of course; Fred Lebow banned them completely*]. I am assured – and I honestly believe – that there is no anti-wheelchair attitude. On the contrary, there are so many people who care very much.
        Yours sincerely …"

Not surprisingly, I found the explanations difficult to accept, pointing out that the reasons given to him for the non-inclusion of wheelchairs were different from the reasons given to us. By then I'd had a further exchange with John Disley (see below) and wrote back quoting the "caring" nature of Disley's remarks in "Running" magazine, as well as the more recent correspondence with him, a copy of "Sharing the Road" and so on. It was all returned, but without a covering note.

I also wrote to Des Lynam, who was the chief commentator for BBC television – again, my letter to him is missing – about the issue, and he also replied, being rather more supportive than anyone else so far, but by this stage unable to do anything:

> "Dear Tim
> Thank you very much for your letter. Had I been aware of the position before the event took place, we might have been able to help, however, I feel it is too late.
>   Yours sincerely…"

And … there *was* a wheelchair athlete in the race, someone called Billy Thornton, well-known to the Stoke Mandeville hierarchy, who had completed the entry form in the usual way and then, somehow, engaged the services of Jimmy Savile to get into the marathon. I don't know the details of how this was done – at what stage in the application–registration–turning-up-on-the-day sequence JS was pulled in. I did find out that the athlete was made to start at the back, but there he was, the first ever wheelchair in the race. So I wrote to Jimmy Savile at "Jim'll Fix it":

> "Dear Jim
> OK, you fixed it for the guy in the wheelchair last Sunday. But did you know that a number of us have been trying to persuade the organisers of the London Marathon to have a proper wheelchair section – established as the British National Wheelchair Marathon? People have completed wheelchair marathons in the following places: Manchester, Birmingham (twice), Guildford, Stockport, Norwich, Wolverhampton, Cardiff and Humber Bridge (at least). How to run a wheelchair section is explained in the May edition of Running magazine (pages 82-83). Can you pull any

strings for next year? I can produce a dozen people who already have faster times than the bloke who did the London course this year.

Best wishes ..."

I didn't hear anything, probably because the letter will have been screened out by the army of production assistants before it reached him.

And then there was the exchange with John Disley. I wrote straight after the race. Actually, I drafted a letter on the Monday, but did a re-draft which was sent on Thursday the 13th, after the first reply from Cliff Morgan:

"Dear John Disley
My apologies for taking things up again quite so soon, but really! A pantomime horse, a three-legged affair, a penny-farthing, roller skates, an ostrich, a pram ... and a wheelchair. More power to his corns, and I am pleased that he finished, but I can produce a dozen people in this country (including at least one woman) who have done far faster times on far harder courses. After last Sunday more extensive wheelchair participation is bound to be attempted next year, and it were far better that it be organised properly than that you try to cope with a bunch of gate-crashing cowboys. In anticipation I am already compiling a ranking list of this season's performances.

I can understand that you have more than enough on your plate without becoming involved with a wheelchair section as well. If the British Sports Association for the Disabled were approached, I am sure they would be willing to organise a wheelchair section limited to (say) the best dozen or so athletes from the previous year.

With best wishes ..."

He replied a week later, on May 21st, though whether this was before or after Cliff Morgan had approached him I don't know. The letter was hand-written, on official London Marathon notepaper:

"Dear Tim Marshall

Thank you for your comments about the 'clowns' in our marathon [*NB I had made no comment about the 'clowns', merely describing either their dress or means of locomotion*].

Although we are not best pleased with ostriches and pantomime horses [*why not? Don't they add to the gaiety of the occasion?*] at least they did not commit perjury when they signed their entry forms, as Mr Thornton apparently did [*perjury? PERJURY! This is getting heavy!*].

Incidentally, we did not permit Mr Thornton to start, we just left him alone, however he did receive a medal at the finish and I believe that our officials were courteous to him.

Next year we will again run our race under IAAF, AAA and WCCA rules which do not admit to wheels of any kind – cycles, prams or chairs.
Yours sincerely
John I Disley"

If I was appalled by his comments in "Running", I was outraged by this letter. The accusation of perjury was almost laughable, had it not been made by someone in such a position of authority in the race. But a wider perspective, taken in conjunction with his comments in "Running" ("not a multi-purpose jamboree") shows a distaste for, and almost a disapproval of, the very people who make his race possible, the thousands of runners both dressed up and not, and of whose fund-raising activities he was so proud. Except for something like a World Championship or an Olympics, the prospect of having the roads closed for several hours for, perhaps, 50 or even 100 elite runners seemed to me pretty thin; and even if it were possible, *they* wouldn't be raising money for a favourite charity.

The immediate next step was to complain to the Minister for Sport about the attitudes revealed by Disley's letter; not for itself, because anyone might validly hold what I regarded as antediluvian views, but because he was Vice-Chairman of the Sports Council whose major slogan was "Sport for All", and the attitudes expressed in the letter seemed incompatible with that. Neil Macfarlane replied six weeks later, on July 23rd, welcoming the efforts the Sports Council had made during the IYDP to increase access to sport for disabled people, but pointing out that it would take some time for "unnecessary barriers" preventing participation to be removed. Almost as an afterthought, he added that John Disley's term of office as Vice-Chairman of the Sports Council had finished on June 30th and was not renewed (he had been a member of the Council for 12 years by then).

The Internationals, Stoke Mandeville 1978: The men's relay

How to load a wheelchair into a Boeing 747. Heathrow, 1978

Cyclops, an early handcycle. Craig Hospital, Denver, August 1978

The attack on Kathy Switzer, Boston Marathon 1967. Credit The Boston Herald

"Brands Hatch comes to Sutton Park" (1). May 1980

"Brands Hatch comes to Sutton Park" (2)

Interlude 1. Challenger, the trimaran

The first Norfolk Marathon - finish. May 1982. © Eastern Daily Press

Interlude 2. Sledging above Chamonix, early 1980s

London Marathon finish, Westminster Bridge 1985

Breathing Space

Away from road-racing for a short while, Sports 'n Spokes now published an article as significant in its own way as "Sharing the Road" had been the previous year. The previous few years had seen the development of a series of what eventually became known as the Diamond League athletics meetings, one- (or more usually two-) day athletics meetings all over Europe and the USA (and latterly in the Middle and Far East as well) show-casing the top athletes in each event, with results from each meeting cumulating to an over-all champion. This is similar to what now happens in rowing, skiing, cycling and no doubt many other sports. Now, there was a series of wheelchair races, between 400 and 1500 metres, inserted into the running events as part of the afternoon's entertainment, in several of the athletics meetings. "Integration", in the track circuit, and absolutely analogous to the road experience, con-sists of staging an event *in parallel* with the able-bodied activity, and placing the wheelchair version of the sport in front of spectators come to view the sport. It can be seen, in a not very subtle way, as part of a public education campaign.

Another example of the same principle occurred around the same time, or maybe a couple of years earlier. Arising from my membership of the Watersports Sub-Committee, Liz Dendy asked me to run the Sports Council's "Canoeing for Disabled People" stand at Crystal Palace National Sports Centre as part of the "Canoe Show" held over a weekend in February or March. The Council produced the literature, the photographs, and the Caranoe, and my role was to sit there explaining to anyone who stopped by about how disabled people could be got canoeing. On one of the occasions I did this I noticed posters all over the centre advertising the forthcoming "Basketball Finals" to be held there shortly. All the preliminary matches had been played earlier, resulting in a final between the two best teams in the country. But not just a one-off match between the two best male teams:

specifically, the poster gave the timetable for different matches: there was the youths' final followed by the women's final followed by the wheelchair final … and so on. You would go to watch these if you were interested in basketball (or, maybe, because you had a relative playing there), and would encounter, maybe for the first time, a version of the sport of which you might have been completely unaware; putting the "disabled" version of the sport in front of a sport-specific audience. At this stage Phil Craven was a very successful international player, and it's likely that he was already getting involved with the administration of the sport. I don't know for certain, but I suspect he had something to do with the outreach of his sport into the public space.

Back to the marathon. The direct approach obviously was going nowhere, and there seemed no point in expecting anything to come from any future approach to B&D; other directions would have to be found. Before re-starting the crusade, however, there was work to be done in the form of more marathons in more places.

I was attracted by the Piccadilly Marathon in June, not least because of its unusual timing. Most races started on Sunday mornings, usually 11 o'clock, though variations on this time were quite common. One consequence of this was that, except for the advent of gales such as had occurred in Norfolk (and were to recur later that year on the Humber Bridge race), air temperatures rose gradually during the race, just as you, the runner, wanted them to fall because *you* were getting warm. But the Piccadilly started at 4 o'clock on the Saturday afternoon, so the air temperature was cooling down as you were warming up.

There was no headstart, so I insinuated myself somewhere near the front of the thousands of runners, taking care not to chop any ankles while the runners became strung out during the early part of the race. I knew nothing of the course beforehand (as was usually the case), but it seemed pretty flat – good for wheelchairs – until about 8 miles in when there was a short, steep climb of maybe half a mile. Lots of runners came past as I slowly pushed up the hill, but the pay-off came immediately after, as the height gained was gradually lost over 3 or 4 miles – an ideal arrangement for wheelchairs, as by now the runners were well-separated and the wheelchair could zip past at 15 mph or even faster.

The rest of the course was pretty flat, memorable mainly for the passage through Moss Side. This area had a dreadful reputation for crime, especially drugs and guns, but pushing through it almost every doorstep had people outside clapping and screaming like mad as we came past *their* house. And then, less than a mile from the finish, who should catch me up but Gerry Kinsella. He must have started further back in the pack than me, but being faster had slowly caught me up. And now here he was, and though I tried to stay with him for the last few hundred yards, he gradually eased ahead to finish in 1 second over 3½ hours, with me 29 seconds behind. This, obviously, was slower than his time on the Humber Bridge the year before, but later this year he lowered his own personal best, and the British record, to 3h 1m on the Mersey Marathon. The 3-hour barrier was getting very close.

I wrote to the organisers afterwards, congratulating them on a brilliant course, and asking them about the possibility of a headstart in future. They replied, thanking me for the comment on the course, but saying that the AAA insisted that where there were wheelchairs in a race, they must start at the back. I never did discover which bit of the organisation had promulgated this advice – rule, even – because it was clearly contrary to what had become routine practice in North America, and to what our limited experience in Britain had already shown was best practice. And I wondered whether the AAA had turned a blind eye to the Great North Run, at whose second running in June Alan Robinson won the wheelchair event for the second time, in 1 hour 32 minutes; or whether they simply didn't know what was going on up there.

The following year, in the pre-race publicity, Alan's achievement occasioned a half-page feature article in the supplement produced by the local newspaper, headed "He's King of the Road". And, as part of the inclusion of wheelchair racing to which such publicity contributed, the official entry form for 1983, in addition to all the usual questions, had a final question which read: "Do you intend to take part in a **self-propelled** wheelchair?" That's all that it took to effect a complete normalisation of the wheelchair section, with the main race administration embracing all the elements needed to run a successful event. (Later, it became obvious that other elements were needed: if you wanted to make the race an international event, there would be the question of arranging accommodation for overseas visitors; and for point-to-point courses, arranging to transport everyday wheelchairs from start to finish; but these were a long way in the future for us.)

Back to business. Mike O'Flynn must have been well in post by now, because he embarked on some correspondence with the AAA over the "ruling" that had emerged over wheelchairs starting behind the runners. Mary Glen Haig ,the BSAD president, who had fenced for the UK as far back as the 1948 Olympics, and who subsequently became a Dame and a full member of the IOC, suggested writing to Arthur Gold, of the European Athletic Association, seeking to enlist his support in changing the ruling. Mike adduced times recorded in both the USA and in Britain.

Arthur Gold (later Sir Arthur) replied, pointing out (correctly) that neither the AAA or the IAAF had any jurisdiction over the running of wheelchair marathons. He agreed that wheelchairs trying to negotiate their way through a crowd of runners in front was not a good idea, but supposed that, with the times reported from the USA, the wheelchairs must surely be geared, "like ten-speed bicycles", and suggesting a direct approach to Squire Yarrow, president of the AAA. Mike replied, disabusing him of the notion of geared wheelchairs, and wrote to the AAA. Squire Yarrow replied stating that the AAA had **not** laid down any specific rules about the conduct of races in which there was a wheelchair section. We never discovered how the contradiction arose, nor whether there was ever any formal guidance issued by the AAA as to the future conduct of races; but the idea of a headstart seemed gradually to be adopted by race organisers all over the country.

From somewhere I had picked up the hint of a view that some people still held that wheelchairs and runners were actually in direct competition, and whichever one of them finished in front had "beaten" the other. We needed to squash this notion fast, or it would severely damage the concept of integrated racing that had been developing. I wasn't in a position, and nor was BSAD, to issue a "decree" to individual athletes or race organisers explaining the "correct" way of looking at things, but I used a back-door approach to try to clear up one angle. Another of my post-graduate students, Paul Gully, from the same cohort as Dee, who had shepherded me round Bassenthwaite, wanted to try a marathon for the first time. We suspected that any race which declared that runners and wheelchairs were in direct competition would automatically be de-recognised as far as the running times were concerned, so I got Paul to write to the IAAF:

> "Dear Sir
> I am considering taking part in a marathon which will be held under IAAF regulations, and as I understand that persons in wheelchairs will be taking part I am wondering whether my time for this event would be regarded as official.
> Yours sincerely ..."

> "Dear Mr Gully
> Thank you for your letter concerning the forthcoming marathon in which you will be participating.
>
> There is nothing in IAAF rules to prevent your time being completely official. We wish you all the best in the competition.
> Yours sincerely ..."

Little by little. The international governing body hadn't expressed any opposition to wheelchair participation, which, apart from the issue of direct or parallel competition, seemed to leave the matter in the hands of individual race organisers.

I discussed how else to pursue the London business with Mike O'Flynn, at the same time as we had decided to go to the AAA and the IAAF. I think it was Liz Dendy who first suggested trying the Greater London Council, then the local authority governing London, and at that time under Labour control (but please keep her name out of it, as a senior officer in the Sports Council). The crucial point here was that the roads used for the race were public roads under the notional control of the Greater London Council, the GLC. If the GLC was known for anything it was for supporting minority or disadvantaged groups: women, ethnic minorities, people with disabilities, and so on. Surely they would at least listen to us?

As with national government, there were two groups of people involved: the politicians and the civil servants; in this context, we're talking about councillors and local government officers. As with all councils, there were different areas of responsibility: Education, Housing, Social Services , and so on. And in London, Arts and Recreation, which included Sport. The chief officer for A&R was Lord Birkett, whilst the chair of the committee, at that time a GLC councillor but not yet an MP, was Tony Banks. And then we discovered that one of the governors of the race was Illtyd Harrington, who was chairman of the GLC and Ken Livingstone's deputy. This all looked promising. The approach to the GLC began in June, and stretched right through to the 1983 race (April 17th) and beyond. Unrealised by us at the start, this contact became a hugely important part of the ultimate denouement, and it seems better to present this aspect of the story as an integrated whole, uninterrupted by other matters going on at the same time, but which were in essence isolated events without a contribution to the main story as it unfolded during the autumn and early new year.

Humber Bridge

I entered the Humber Bridge race with the explicit intent to break Gerry Kinsella's time of 3h 15m set the year before. (At this point I don't think I'd heard of his time in the Mersey Marathon.) The course looked quite good, starting at the western edge of the city, going west along the A63 to the bridge, then once over that turning south-east towards Grimsby. Alas, just as in the Norfolk marathon, the weather was foul, only even worse than Norfolk, with a wild southerly gale and slashing rain most of the way. I didn't even break 4 hours, let alone the 3 I'd hoped for, and so retreated, somewhat chastened, back to the Midlands. It was the last race of the year for me.

Ullswater

But not quite the last event. Stephen had been working on the Ullswater problem. He ascertained that I had a canoe (the Caranoe, which I still had on loan from BSAD and which they didn't call back until 1984). Sarah, who had seen me round Thirlmere back on New Year's Day in 1981, was willing to act as part of a canoe escort, and she brought her boyfriend along to help. Stephen, who had wide contacts in the world of outdoor recreation, arranged for a couple of his canoeist friends to be part of the party, too. So the plan was for the canoeists to assemble at first light at Howtown, halfway down the east side of the lake, and to paddle across the south-east corner to the shingle beach at Glenridding. There, Stephen and Wendy would be waiting with the Hofmeister wheelchair, which I would hop into, and then we would proceed much as we had round Windermere: Wendy in the car and Stephen with me on the road, stopping every so often for refreshments.

It was nearly a disaster before we started. Sarah lived in a village just north of Leeds, her place being the last stop before taking off for Stephen's in Kendal (to drop the Hofmeister wheelchair). The Caranoe was tied on to my roof-rack with bungees, lots of them, with the open cockpit uppermost. It was a very gusty afternoon, with the van frequently being buffeted by side-winds. At the northern end of the Doncaster by-pass there was an extra-strong gust and I had a vision of something being blown across the motorway. Someone behind flashed their lights energetically, so I stopped, got out – and discovered there was no Caranoe on the roof. It had been blown off the roof-rack, across the north-bound carriageway, the central reservation, and the south-bound carriageway, onto the verge and down an embankment, all without touching any other vehicle travelling in either direction. It would have been at the perfect height for smashing into the side of a south-bound coach, had one been passing at the right time...

At least two vehicles on the north-bound side had stopped, as had one on the other carriageway who had seen what had happened. Apart from the potential disaster which by some miracle I had escaped, I presumed that I'd have to continue to the end of the by-pass, go right round the roundabout and take the south-bound carriageway, stop by the embankment and, using the man who had stopped on that side, pick up the Caranoe, proceed southwards to the next exit, turn right round again and come back up north. Not a bit of it. The two men on the north-bound side ran across the motorway – both carriageways – to meet up with the man on the south-bound side, retrieve the Caranoe from the embankment down which it had been blown, carry it up to road level, then run across both carriageways with the Caranoe, before shoving it into the van and saying goodbye. I'd had to get into the van first, because I couldn't get in once the Caranoe was in (and similarly, if I were in before the Caranoe was put in, I couldn't get out). At Sarah's, the Caranoe was tied much more firmly onto the roof-rack, and I left for Kendal (to drop the Hofmeister) while Sarah and boyfriend went directly to Howtown. They had already turned in when I arrived.

It was a wild night, with a lot of rain and gusting wind buffeting the side of the van, so I didn't sleep very well. And in the morning, when we were expecting a couple of canoeist friends of Stephen to turn up – nothing, no one. The weather had calmed down a lot since overnight, and after waiting as long as we dared, the three of us set off, before it was fully light. The journey across wasn't too bad – I remember having to raft up on a couple of occasions, but neither lasted very long – and as we approached the beach at Glenridding, there seemed to be quite a large reception party, certainly more than just Stephen and Wendy.

And indeed, there were more, including the two canoeists whom we had expected to be paddling with us across the lake. Early in the morning they had together decided that no one would be daft enough to try to paddle across the lake in those conditions, especially not a disabled person, so they hadn't set out. (I never thought to ask them what on earth was the point of coming to the beach if they didn't think anyone would be paddling across.) They were extremely embarrassed, as well they might have been. Anyway, after a brief stop – I had switched from the Caranoe directly into the Hofmeister (my everyday chair was back in the van at Howtown), some refreshments and saying goodbye to Sarah and boyfriend – I set off with Stephen and Wendy.

The road along the west side of Ullswater is quite narrow and twisty. From time to time there is a lay-by on the lake side of the road, where the road has been slightly straightened (rather as an ox-bow lake is formed). Stephen was quite busy slowing down/fending off cars coming from behind, where the road bent left round a bluff, obscuring sight of the road ahead – and me from behind. But there were straight sections, and at one point a few miles up the road, a Rolls Royce Silver Shadow in British Racing Green glided elegantly past – with a beautiful, polished, wooden full-sized Canadian canoe strapped to a roof-rack. Not a sight you would expect to see, anywhere.

Round the next corner, there was a lake-side lay-by with the Rolls Royce parked in it, and in the middle of the road a stocky, bearded man gesturing frantically at us to go into the lay-by, so we did. The same question flashed both ways: "Who are you, and what are you doing here?" We thought we had an easy explanation, but he? He was called Jack van der Molen, owner and proprietor of a medical equipment and supplies company; to judge from the car, the company was evidently doing very well! His interest in canoeing? He had kayaked for many years, though getting older had meant switching from kayaks to the canoe; but at least it was still possible to get out on the water. And his son, Paul, was an expedition kayaker, and sometimes worked with disabled people facilitating their getting on the water. He had, for example, designed a special paddle for use by people with only one functioning arm. I don't remember why we didn't exchange contact details at the time, but we didn't, and after an unusual refreshment stop, carried on to Pooley Bridge and down the side road to Howtown. The Caranoe had been taken round by Stephen's friends and tied – securely – onto the roof-rack, with the paddle laid on the ground underneath the van. Fortunately, it was still there when we turned up, so I was ready to leave for home as soon as we reached Howtown. Thanks to Stephen and Wendy and … what next? From somewhere – the grapevine, as usual – I learned that Gerry Kinsella had been at it again, this time doing the Long Trip – Lands End–John o' Groats – fund-raising for Greenbank, of course. As is often the case, though, the source didn't reveal how long it had taken him.

We Are The Champions

Ron Pickering first came to public attention as the coach of Lynn Davies, who won the Olympic long jump title in 1964 in Tokyo. He slowly moved away from being a full-time athletics coach to fronting BBC sports programmes on television, especially athletics. Then in 1973 the BBC established a programme called "We are the Champions" (long before the Queen hit song using the same words) in which there were competitions between schools based on a traditional British school sports day, but including water-based events as well. Ron was in overall charge, acting as a kind of compere for the occasion. The format ran until 1991 when Ron died, with his role subsequently being taken on by Gary Lineker for a few years, until the whole programme stopped in 1995. In one sense it was a bit like "It's a Knockout", only for school kids and a lot more serious.

I don't know quite how the disability side of things came to be involved, but someone somewhere suggested that there should be a competition between special schools for physically disabled children. BSAD became involved, and Ivor Mitchell, recently retired as head teacher of one of the special schools in Birmingham, and a BSAD vice-president, identified schools from the West Midlands who could compete against each other. One of the features of the programme was that, each time, a couple of well-known sportsmen or women provided a link between different events, announcing the scores achieved by different schools in the most recent event, introducing the next event, and so on. Mitch asked if I would be willing to take on this role, and put my name forward for one of the two positions. Though I was far from being well-known in the disability sports world, and certainly not for being excellent at anything, the BBC accepted the nomination. I thought it might just offer an opportunity to make a point to Ron, off camera, about wheelchairs and marathons. (In the end, it didn't.)

The other person chosen for this "link" role was Janet Yates, an able-bodied archer from Northern Ireland whose main claim to fame was that she had lost the 1982 Commonwealth ladies Archery title in a shoot-out against Neroli Fairhall of New Zealand; and Neroli Fairhall was a paraplegic, a wheelchair user. I hadn't heard of Janet before the event, and didn't keep in contact after, but the example her experience provided was a wonderful tool to be used when teaching about disability sport and integration: who is "disability sport" for? and (why) do we need separate competitions for able-bodied and disabled people? (It depends on both the sport and the disability, of course.)

Anyway, we recorded the programme in, I think, the autumn of 1982, though the final edited version wasn't shown until early summer of 1983, by which time I had acquired a certain notoriety over campaigning for London. It was a surprise to be asked to be photographed alongside the kids, both those who were competing and those who were just spectators from the participating schools. And signing autograph books ...

The Second Battle of Marathon
The Greater London Council

I drafted a letter to the GLC, to Tony Banks, on June 9th. In it, I suggested that it was more than time for London to include a wheelchair section in its marathon, citing examples both from overseas: Boston, Rotterdam, Berlin, Paris and others; and in this country: Manchester, Birmingham, Wolverhampton, Hull and so on; and suggesting that our event might be called "The GLC London Wheelchair Marathon". The rationale for including information about events elsewhere was, of course, the implication that London was falling behind, not only other big international cities, but also provincial cities in this country, cities which could hardly claim to have the same status as London. I did also mention that Brasher and Disley were implacably opposed, but without suggesting why this might be so.

For some reason it was never sent – I think I probably had second thoughts about the likelihood of a letter from an unknown individual successfully hitting the target. So I sent this draft to Mike, along with my recent article in "Running" magazine and Disley's reply, and various other letters and items of information including my letter to the Minister (his reply came six weeks later). The same day, BSAD centrally sent out a letter to their regions (chairmen, secretaries and officers) asking them to collect and collate any information they could acquire about wheelchair marathons being done in their regions, and to send the information to me. The idea was to circulate a list of races and times at the end of the year.

From this point the correspondence is incomplete, but enough remains to provide more than a mere skeleton of what happened. A letter from Mike at the end of the June suggested meeting in July, and included the news that Philip Lewis, a full member of the Sports Council and shortly to become BSAD national chairman (or who *was* chairman and was about to relinquish the post), had had a "discussion" with Disley about the matter, pressing the wheelchair case very strongly; but that Disley was still muttering on about perjury. The letter to Tony Banks, from Mike, finally went out on July 29th, including a formal proposal to stage the first National Wheelchair Marathon in association with the 1983 London Marathon. The proposal included details of who the organiser should be (BSAD, of course), the numbers of entrants (20), and suggestions for the start (10 minutes' headstart), refreshments and finish. The letter was copied to me, and gave me the label of "National Wheelchair Marathon Coordinator", a designation I was happy to use thereafter.

Whilst we waited for Tony Banks to reply, I had another thought: the race was called "The Gillette London Marathon", because Gillette were putting up the sponsorship money. How about trying to interest them? But, again, what would be the point of a letter from me? I floated the idea to Mike, who, as it happened, knew the UK national chairman of the company, and he sent off a letter outlining the state of wheelchair marathoning both in Britain and abroad, suggesting that they might like to add a string to their bow in supporting "The Gillette London Wheelchair Marathon", admitting the opposition of Brasher and Disley, but hinting at the interest of the GLC (see below). I don't know what happened to the approach to Gillette – it seems to have gone up a blind alley. I have no more correspondence from or to them, and I recall no discussion about them at all. Possibly, having been alerted to the opposition to a wheelchair section, they decided that they didn't want to fish in such murky waters, and simply declined to become involved at all.

The GLC had replied on September 9th, from Peter Pitt (Tony Banks' deputy), inviting Mike to send a list of possible dates for a meeting. A meeting was eventually agreed for early October, and though Mike couldn't attend, he suggested that Jenny Ward, the BSAD officer for the Greater London area, should attend in his stead, along with me. After all, if this lead eventually went somewhere, it was likely that she would be involved with any administrative fall-out to do with organising a wheelchair section. Maybe, just maybe, we were beginning to get somewhere.

That first meeting with the GLC was on Tuesday 5th October. Tony Banks was there, as were Peter Pitt and Lord Birkett, but not Illtyd Harrington. Jenny Ward was also along and she, living and working in London for the

BSAD and with a direct line into headquarters (yes, I know, it's beginning to sound like a military operation, but at times that's what it felt like), became an important link drawing things together. I remember little about the meeting, except that I presented an abbreviated account of wheelchair marathons, initially in the USA and then over here, and ending up with the proposal Mike had sent at the end of July. Both Banks and Pitt expressed strong support for the idea, but wanted a specific London slant to the event; so, on the hoof, Jenny and I suggested that the original proposal for 20 participants be modified to 10 from Greater London and 10 from elsewhere. This seemed acceptable but, deferring to the absent Illtyd Harrington, who was both their political senior as well as being a governor of the race, they said I would need to write to him making the full case. I left several papers with Pitt, including the recent correspondence with Disley; but even before they had a chance to read it, I picked up from Banks a considerable antipathy towards Chris Brasher. Maybe this was a kind of perverted wishful thinking on my part, but the same antipathy was evident at all subsequent meetings. Jenny and I left the meeting in high spirits, believing that we had found the key to what had up until now been a firmly closed and locked door. Each of us wrote to Mike the next day with our impressions of the meeting, again full of optimism.

The letter to Illtyd Harrington went the next day. I included a copy of "Sharing the Road" from "Sports 'n Spokes", a recent article from the same source on the Montreal Marathon showing an application of the rationale for integrated racing, the article by me that had appeared in "Running" magazine, and the proposal for establishing a race with 20 entrants, modified to make explicit it would be for 10 athletes from London and 10 from elsewhere. I added that Tony Banks and Peter Pitt were in favour (this had come over very strongly at the meeting), but that Brasher and Disley were opposed, notwithstanding approaches going back three years. Finally, I offered to meet him to discuss the matter further, if he was interested; and waited.

But not for long. The meeting had been on October 5th, and my letter to Illtyd Harrington went on the 6th. He replied on the 8th, thus:

"Dear Tim Marshall

Thank you for your note regarding a wheelchair section in the London Marathon.

I am in contact with Peter Pitt to try and organise a meeting and would be very happy to meet you. I will be in touch as soon as we sort out a date and time.

I have also copied your letter to Chris Brasher who is, as you know, the Co-ordinator.
    Yours sincerely…"

He sent me a copy of his letter to Brasher, the last paragraph of which read: "I have discussed this with Sir James Swaffield, my fellow governor, this afternoon and he is as keen as I am that we get this proposition before the governors as quickly as possible. I attach some relevant papers."

The date on the letter is indistinct, but it was sent in late October or very early November.

Quite rightly, I don't have a copy of Brasher's reply, nor of what transpired at the meeting of the governors, though each would be fascinating.

The next letter from Illtyd Harrington was dated November 15th:

"Dear Tim Marshall

Further to my last letter of 8th November, I now write to invite you to a meeting with Peter Pitt and myself, on Tuesday 30th November 30th at 3 p.m.

Could you please confirm if this is convenient…
    Yours sincerely…"

On the 17th Mike wrote asking if I was going to select the athletes for the race, or whether he should make the necessary arrangements. Then Jenny wrote asking if I had a definite outcome about London. News was leaking out – in truth, rumour rather than news – and they were receiving lots of enquiries from prospective entrants. The region had agreed to hold a race, a kind of elimination event, in the Docklands on Saturday 18th December, a two-lap half-marathon from which the top 10 would be selected as London's entrants; and because she, Jenny, was going to be in Austria at the time, the event would be co-ordinated and run by Julia Allton, a senior lecturer in PE from Tower Hamlets Institute of Adult Education, together with an army of volunteer helpers.

This was all going a bit fast. Yes, I was pleased about the Docklands race, even though the roads wouldn't be closed (though Saturday in the Docklands would, I supposed, be pretty free of traffic); but the GLC had *not* (yet) agreed to there being a wheelchair race as part of the main event the following April – many others were involved in making such a decision. Looking further ahead I suggested to Mike that, if the GLC couldn't eventually swing it, BSAD put on a press conference to expose the whole business, and that we offer the event, the First National Wheelchair Marathon, to the Piccadilly race (because this was by far the best course I'd yet been on). This would, of course, have to be cleared with them first, rather than just announcing it. Meantime...

An Unexpected Threat

In mid-November, at work, the phone rang.

"Hello, Tim Marshall."

"Mr Marshall, I understand you organise marathons for wheelchairs." A woman's voice, very Welsh.

"Well, not exactly, I try to find out what's going on, what races people have done, what their times were, what the course was like, and then tell everyone else what's going on."

"Oh good," she said, "because we're going to put on the first national wheelchair marathon next year, just for wheelchairs, and we would like to invite you to join the organising committee."

Alarm bells began to ring. Right from the start I'd been worried that someone, no doubt very well-intentioned, would stage a wheelchair-only marathon that would encapsulate a view offering a completely different perspective on wheelchair road-racing: *"Ah, isn't that nice, they've got their own race,"* and leading to a view that separate races were the right way to do things. I didn't want to be part of my "own race", I wanted to be part of everyone else's race, just as they did in the USA and Canada, reported every two months in "Sports 'n Spokes". And the experience of the last two years had shown that a) it was possible to do that in Britain, and that b) by and large, race organisers were happy to have wheelchairs as part of their event, though there was still some education to do over front-end starts.

I needed to find out more. What organisation was she representing? I couldn't imagine that it was BSAD – surely, Mike O'Flynn would have told me if the hierarchy was planning something like this? The only other organisation I could think of was the British Paraplegic Sports Society – the BPSS, which I wasn't in favour of, because they limited their eligibility to spinal injury people only; and in any case, there hadn't been a squeak out of them about marathoning over the previous two years. So…

"What organisation are you from? When's the race going to be, and where? But perhaps you haven't got that far yet."
"It doesn't matter what organisation I'm from, but," her voice dropped to a conspiratorial tone, "I can assure you that there are some very, very important people involved." An even more hushed tone. "Downing Street is interested."

If that were true, it would be quite likely to sink any widespread interest in integrated marathons for some time, certainly as far as London was concerned. She continued: "But the other matters you asked about: it's going to be held in Hyde Park, in September, and there'll be laps. And there'll be teams of Department of Health engineers round the course, together with pits for servicing the chairs and making any necessary repairs to the chairs as the race unfolds."

"But people don't use Department of Health wheelchairs for racing."
"Oh," she said, evidently quite puzzled. "*Are* there any other kinds of wheelchair?"

In the immortal words of the "News of the World" in a rather different context, I made my excuses and left. But I still hadn't found out what organisation lay behind the plan.

The explanation came in a copy letter from Mike, together with a copy of a letter he had received back in November from Jim Russell. This was the same Jim Russell who had taken part in the People's Marathon 18 months earlier, completing the race in 4 hours 50 minutes, and who had done at least one marathon since (I think), though I knew neither the place nor time. Now, he revealed that Motability was planning to stage the first National Wheelchair Marathon in September 1983. (Motability was – and is – an organisation which acquires new cars at a discounted price and leases them to disabled people in exchange for what used to be called their Mobility Allowance.) There were to be three events: one for children, one for electric wheelchairs, and a full-length marathon for self-propelled wheelchairs. The purpose of this event was three-fold: "To raise funds for Motability and other participating charities; to heighten public awareness of Motability's work; and to bring their variety and development [*of wheelchairs*], as well as the skills necessary in handling them, into sharper focus". (Note the absence, other than in the overall title, of any idea of competition; it would seem to be mainly an event promoting Motability.) In pursuit of all this, would he, Mike O'Flynn, send the number of people in wheelchairs in each of the BSAD regions, and the proportion of these who would be potential participants. As a carrot, he added "Mr Jimmy Savile has accepted Motability's invitation to be associated with the Marathon."

One comment worth making here is that, with the well-known exception of Gerry Kinsella and the Greenbank project, most people (wheelchair athletes) didn't do marathons with the purpose of raising funds (except, perhaps, to buy a proper racing chair for themselves), but rather, just to do them. No one would have expected Hugh Jones or Joyce Smith, our top British runners at the time, to have as their main reason for running to raise funds for a favourite charity through sponsorship, or even to buy a better pair of running shoes; why should wheelchair athletes be any different?

Two months later, on January 28th, Mike wrote a stalling reply (at that stage, we were still hopeful of getting into London), suggesting that Jim Russell contact me about the proposed "National Wheelchair Marathon". I never heard anything more, from either Jim or Motability, and as far as I know no Motability-sponsored event ever took place.

The Greater London Council
(continued)

I went to the meeting on 30th November but remember absolutely nothing about it. The only clue lies in what happened afterwards: there is a copy of a letter I sent to Tony Banks on December 3rd (only Harrington and Pitt had been present, and maybe Birkett; probably, they suggested I write to Banks as a matter of protocol). In it, on behalf of BSAD, I thanked him for the meeting with the others; assured him that with the imminent breakthrough on a wheelchair section we would make sure the GLC was given full credit for this; recognised that there was still a meeting of the governors to take place; and said that we would set in train various administrative arrangements in order that, when confirmation finally came through, we would already have done as much as possible to minimise the additional burden we would have created. This was copied to Harrington and Pitt as well as Mike and Jenny.

There were two further letters from Jenny, on December 7th and 16th, the first being largely about administrative matters but including the important information that a week earlier LBC radio had announced that the GLC were inviting 20 wheelchairs to take part in the inaugural London Wheelchair Marathon. This broadcast had led to Jenny putting a short item in the regional newsletter about the 20 places for wheelchairs in the race, of which 10 would be reserved for athletes from London, and the two news items together provoked a flurry of enquiries to the local office. Someone must have been in touch with Jenny – not me – and told her that things were not so far advanced. So, almost as soon as the newsletter went out, the information about a wheelchair section had to be withdrawn. At this stage, all she could do was to back-track onto the strict *status quo*: that a wheelchair section had yet to be confirmed, but there was a race in the Docklands on the 18th, a race which would become a qualifying race if a wheelchair race as part of London was eventually confirmed.

The second letter, on December 16ᵗʰ, was rather more interesting. It included an account of her meeting Chris Brasher at a conference on Sport in the Community which had been organised by … Peter Pitt; Chris Brasher chaired it. Here is the meat of the letter:

"It was not until after the conference I got the chance to talk to Chris Brasher about wheelchair entrants in the London Marathon in any detail, though I had raised it from the floor. Chris had only just received the letter from the GLC, and was able to explain to me that it would be impossible for wheelchairs to precede the race in 1983. The timing is such that the first runners arrive at Buckingham Palace just as the Changing of the Guard has finished; this is apparently a shortened version following a special dispensation from the palace. The whole race runs on such a tight schedule then, including the closure of a motorway exit, that it would be impossible to have an earlier start for wheelchair entrants in 1983. If this is going to be achieved in 1984 it would seem that this can only happen: 1) if BSAD works towards this end now and it would seem sensible for Michael O'Flynn to make a formal approach to Chris Brasher. 2) For 1983 the best we could hope for is wheelchair entrants at the back or you may think it preferable to seek another venue for the BSAD National Marathon. Chris suggested the one in the Lake District …" [*this was Windermere*]

There are many comments to make about this. Firstly, the speed of transmission of the letter from Illtyd Harrington to the race HQ: about 6 weeks!! Secondly, the argument about the timing of the race in relation to the Changing of the Guard: this was absolutely not relevant to wheelchairs at the time. No one in this country had yet broken 3 hours, and a 10-minute headstart would be likely to result in the leading runners overtaking the leading wheelchairs well before reaching the Tower on the way back out of Docklands. Thus the runners would still have been the first to reach The Mall, and the sanctity of the Changing of the Guard preserved. It was to be several years before the wheelchair times in London became such that, say, a 10-minute front-end start needed an extra dispensation – but by then, other matters had moved the whole argument on. Regarding the closure of a motorway exit I couldn't really comment, since I didn't know which exit was being referred to, but it seemed unlikely that a 10-minute headstart would have been critical. I never had the opportunity to put the case face to face.

Thirdly, the suggestion about starting at the back: bad, bad idea, for obvious reasons (and wouldn't they have to keep the motorway junction closed for longer than if opening it earlier for a headstart?) In any case, Brasher and Disley could hardly complain that there wasn't time to incorporate a wheelchair section, since the first approach to them had been over three years ago and one way or another I had been sniping at them ever since (and, as it turned out, so had others, though not for quite so long). On the other hand, the letter seemed to show a greater openness to the idea of a wheelchair race, opening the possibility of a 1984 event rather than Disley's "in a few years time ...", and without any suggestion that it might "... erode the quality of the race." But now, to judge from the enquiries to Jenny's office, and the letters and phone calls I was getting, a head of steam was building up that would be extremely difficult to defuse by telling everyone that a London wheelchair event would be held next year, not this ("jam tomorrow, but not today"). I don't think anyone took the Windermere suggestion seriously.

So the Docklands event took place, not exactly a half marathon, but 12.56 miles. Julia Allton sent me the results, which I have managed to lose, but one bit of paperwork which does exist still revealed that the winner had taken "just over an hour". If this were true, it was an astonishing time, suggesting that a full marathon might have been done in less than 2½ hours, over 30 minutes faster than any time yet achieved in Britain, and threatening our argument for a front-end start which would not blow open the carefully arranged compromise with the Palace. The full results would have clarified all that, but although it looks menacing through the retrospectroscope, I don't remember feeling alarmed at the time, so the "just over an hour" report is probably putting a generous gloss on things.

Then I heard from a contact in County Hall that there was a certain amount of opposition to the idea of a wheelchair section altogether. The nature of this information, who had leaked/released it, I didn't know: none of the existing paperwork says anything about this, but there is enough to indicate that the concern was on grounds of safety. I wrote immediately to Illtyd Harrington, enclosing quotes from various US athletes following the banning of wheelchairs from the New York marathon in 1979. The material covered both the principle and practice of wheelchair participation. I acknowledged that most of the names would be unknown to a British audience, except for Bill Rogers, who was then one of the greatest marathon runners of all time. And I finished with the following: "Why is it safe to have 61 wheelchairs amongst 20,000 runners in the Great North Run (the numbers in 1982), but dangerous to have 20 wheelchairs amongst 18,000 runners in the London Marathon?"

There was more correspondence from Jenny to both Brasher and Disley, urging them to consider establishing a wheelchair race in 1984 – and to announce it – though I have no reply to either. Then in the middle of January, Mike O'Flynn wrote again to Illtyd Harrington:

"Dear Mr Harrington
I would be very interested to know whether you have received a reply from the organisers of the Gillette London Marathon because we are now getting rather impatient enquiries from our prospective wheelchair entrants.

If any problems have occurred I am sure they can be overcome with goodwill.

I would be happy to attend a meeting with you and the organisers so that hopefully we can sort out any objections which may have been raised…"

At around the same time I was sent a cutting from the London evening paper, the "Evening Standard", which reported that I had proposed to Chris Brasher that 20 wheelchair athletes should be included in the 1983 race, at that point exactly 3 months away. The cutting was undated, and I don't know who sent it. I wrote immediately to the Standard, setting out the situation as I then knew it, denying that I (or anyone else, as far as I knew) was in negotiations with Brasher and Disley, and acknowledging that though discussions were going on, I wasn't at liberty to say who was involved.

I ended up with the same final paragraph I had sent to Illtyd Harrington not long before, contrasting the enlightened views of those in the north-east with those in London. I neither sought nor expected a reply, and wasn't disappointed.

What appeared to be the final blow came in a letter from Illtyd Harrington to Mike O'Flynn dated February 2nd:

"Dear Mr O'Flynn
We have now been able to take advice following the discussions we had previously and I am afraid that the answer is that the organisers cannot let wheelchair entrants into the London Marathon.

There are two reasons for this:

1. The event is run under IAAF rules and competitors using wheels are debarred
2. Experience in other mass marathons has shown that wheelchair entrants are dangerous to other competitors.

Tony, Peter and myself are far from happy and if there is any way you feel that we can get round this, please let me know.
    Yours sincerely …"

Mike replied two days later:

"Dear Mr Harrington,
I was obviously extremely disappointed to receive your letter dated February 2nd 1983 and I have consulted with our President, Mrs Mary Glen Haig, CBE who was chairman of the CCPR for five years and is still an Executive Member. I hope she will be able to help but will keep you informed.
    With best wishes
    Yours sincerely …"

A week later I wrote to Illtyd Harrington, addressing him by his first name, which can only be because either he had sent me a letter (which I didn't keep) in which he had called me Tim, or because he had rung me at work and we'd had a conversation on first-name terms, or because at the last meeting he suggested using first names; the last seems the most likely explanation.

"Dear Illtyd,
Mike O'Flynn sent me a copy of your letter of last week – depressing news, though I think I'd half expected it. I did warn you (or rather , Tony Banks) in the original proposal that there was "bitter opposition" from "the organisers". I guess you found it.

I'm writing this in a personal capacity, without my BSAD official hat on, but there is nevertheless something you can do, and this is to send me a list of "The Governors" of the race and of "The Organisers" if they are different. [*Probably wisely, and certainly correctly, he never did.*]

With respect to the specific excuses (you may have occasion to discuss these somewhere or other):

1. IAAF rules. I have a letter from the IAAF secretariat in which it is stated that the presence of wheelchair athletes in/among an IAAF-authorised event in no way de-officialises the times recorded by runners.

    The "rule" is only a problem if wheelchair athletes are perceived as taking part in the same event as runners (this is why, you will recall, the proposal was put for the wheelchair event to be held "in conjunction with" the London Marathon). If, on the other hand, they are perceived as taking part in their own event which happens to be going on at the same time ...

    Another IAAF rule is that men and women may not take part in the same event. Anyone of sound mind can see that the wheelchair athletes are very much competing on wheels against the runners, quite contrary to the regulations, whereas it is plain for all to see that the fact that men and women runners start in the same place, at the same time, run along the same course, and finish in the same place, <u>in no way</u> means they are taking part in the same race. Truly, the emperor's new clothes are indeed wonderful! [*This, I think, was the first time I thought of this particular perspective on the then current practice; it was to be useful two weeks later when I let fly with another salvo.]*

2. Safety. There was, I believe, an incident in the New York marathon 6 or 7 years ago, and of course Brasher has used that race as a model for London. However, I know of no incident since in the USA, and none at all in Britain. With the example of the Great North Run (20,000 runners, 61 wheelchairs), one must suppose that "the organisers" of London imagine that the runners, or the wheelchair athletes, or (just possibly) "the organisers " themselves are less competent than those up north.

One more point. It is of course dangerous to have 16,000 runners jostling along a road all bunched together – perhaps you might suggest to "the organisers" that the whole event is dangerous and should be scrapped! Seriously though, it may appear to be dangerous, but if organised properly as we proposed, it is not. I would again demand that Brasher produce his evidence.

I gather Mike O'Flynn is beavering away behind the scenes hoping to put more pressure on, but I don't give much for his chances. When that comes to a full stop, we shall have to consider again how to proceed; the only thing that won't happen is that the whole issue will be dropped.

Thanks again for your interest and support.
    Yours sincerely ..."

It really did seem like the end of the road. I couldn't think of any different, let alone higher, authority to whom we could appeal. The last letter, to Illtyd, was written in part in desperation, and I just hoped he didn't construe it as a menacing threat to the whole event. Had I waited another week, I probably wouldn't have included the last two paragraphs, but it had gone, and that was that.

The Third Battle of Marathon

The situation looked pretty desperate. Marathons were being done all over the country with wheelchair participants, and there was the supreme example of the Great North Run, but from London, a flat refusal. The Greater London Council seemed powerless to intervene, having been caught on the "it's against international regulations" hook. And there was a threat – for I saw it as such – of a "special" race just for wheelchairs being staged in Hyde Park organised by Motability who, although not known for their interest in sport, were certainly a big player in a wider aspect of disability issues. But this wasn't offering the kind of integrated model that I was interested in, and which was happening everywhere else, or so it seemed. Could the BSAD hierarchy outface Motability? Would it want to, or would it sling its hook and offer to join in with them? Troubled times indeed.

Things began to change when three matters came together to provide a key which finally began to unlock things. A friend, knowing I was interested in wheelchair road-racing, showed me a page from "Running" magazine. Amidst lots of advertisements for road races here, there and everywhere, there was one which stood out as being slightly different. "Man against Horse," it proclaimed, "under AAA laws". Man against horse??!! Under AAA laws???

It turned out that this event, which had been going for some years already (and, as I write this 33 years later, still is), at Llanwrtyd Wells in the Welsh borders, indeed had men running against horses. The course was about 22 miles across country (there may have been some road involvement as well), and after the men had started they were followed some 20 minutes later by horses (each with a rider, of course) whose aim was to catch and overtake the runners before the finish line was reached. (I believe that, up to and including the 1982 event, the horses had always "won" – that is, crossed the finishing line first). But how could this be said to be taking place "under

AAA laws"? – unless runners and horses were actually taking part in separate events run in parallel? Men and horses … Hmmm.

It has been a rule of the IAAF that men and women do not compete against each other in athletics. Both sexes may take part in a single meeting, but whether running, jumping or throwing, the two sexes do not compete directly. (As an aside, you might like to consider in which sports there *is* direct competition. The only two I have found are gliding and equestrianism – show jumping and eventing – in which you might have thought that the strength needed to control half a ton of horse would put women at a considerable disadvantage; but apparently not.) Whilst it is easy to see the sexual segregation in track and field athletics, it isn't so obvious on the road. Major events like the Great North Run and the London Marathon often have different starting times for elite men and women, and sometimes different starting places, but the mass of runners seem to start at the same time and place irrespective of sex.

It is different, however, at the finish. For the early finishers, in major televised races you often see long tapes held by race officials stretching out for twenty yards or more from a finishing chute to channel the runners into specific finishing funnels. The tapes are swung to and fro according to the sex of the runner, so that men and women – the elite runners, at least – are seen to finish in different funnels and the fiction that men and women are taking part in different races may be maintained. Men and women … OK.

(And now, in 2017, there are reportedly discussions taking place within the IAAF (and FINA, the international governing body for swimming) about the possibility of having mixed- sex relay races.

Much like the Olympics and the IOC, amateurism was a totem pole before which the IAAF genuflected – and made all its member organisations conform, too. It was even in its title – the International *Amateur* Athletics Federation. (It is worth noting that, since the advent of, in effect, fully professionalised athletics, the organisation has kept the initials but changed the words: it is now the International *Association* of Athletics Federations. The change was effected in 1992, and two years later the IAAF moved its headquarters from Richmond, in south-west London, to Monaco; well, who wouldn't? But its location in Richmond made it easy to get to for any British investigative journalist interested in the politics of the sport of athletics). This meant that no professional athlete could take part in any event run under the aegis of the IAAF, or its member organisations. If they did, all the amateur athletes taking part would have had their amateur status compromised, and they would be disqualified from taking part in any IAAF-accredited events in future – including the most prestigious of them all, the Olympic Games.

One of the remarkable features of this ruling was that it did not apply only to amateur athletes taking part with professional athletes. Amateur athletes could not take part in *any* sports event in which professional sportsmen or women from *any* sport were also taking part. So, if a professional footballer, or boxer, or ... (you name the sport) were to take part in a fun-run, perhaps raising money for a favourite charity, all the other runners would be automatically disqualified from any and all IAAF-authorised events in future – including, of course, all the top amateur runners who might have been invited to the event in the first place. It is fair to say that by this time the IAAF had taken a somewhat relaxed view over the co-participation in road-racing of professional sports men and women from other sports. Not so the AAA.

Back in December 1982 "Running" magazine had a savage editorial on the consequences of the rigorous application of the amateurism rule, which it is worth quoting at length:

> "The source of the problem is a minority of runners ... [*they*] are the professionals from other sports who enhance the publicity and prestige of races like the London, who give their fellow runners an extra thrill when they line up alongside them and who often raise large amounts of money for charity.

> The problem is that the AAA says professionals are taboo. No matter that the AAA has chosen to turn a blind eye to its own rules for the last two Londons; ... no matter that only weeks ago the sport finally declared itself semi-pro at the top level [*this referred to the IAAF allowing the creation of Trust Funds for athletes to put winnings into, to be drawn on for expenses incurred in racing, and to be fully accessed after retirement*] ... in

some mysterious way everyone who lined up alongside Kevin Keegan in the 1981 Great North Run, or with Alan Minter in the 1982 London, was defiled by their presence. Were you aware that it's a sin to speak to Jimmy Savile? After all, he once competed in pro cycle races and that makes him illegal too. Will the AAA refuse to let *him* run next year?

... [*Mike*] Farrell, General Secretary of the AAA, says that Hugh Jones could theoretically be banned from the World Championships if he won London and John Conteh, say, was in the same race. This assumes that other countries have armies of officials all as dedicated to nitpicking as some of Britain's appear to be. It also ignores the fact that Hugh Jones and hundreds of other top runners should have been banned long ago for similar offences in the past. (Jones won the last London wearing a vest advertising a shoe company – also against the rules).

This merely highlights that the AAA has lost control, and that many of its rules are stupid and unenforceable. They are also out of step with international thinking on the subject."

There was more, castigating the incompetence of the AAA in attempting to enforce rules dating back to Victorian times and the era of high amateurism, whilst simultaneously managing to fall out of step with their own international governing body, which was at last beginning to move with the times.

I knew nothing of any representations made by British race organisers to the IAAF about this matter, nor whether a similar problem arose in other countries where mass fun-running was becoming part of the normal sporting spectrum. Suffice it to say that, in very short order, the IAAF changed its rules to allow professional sportsmen and women from any sport other than athletics to take part in fun-runs and the like, without sanctions against amateur runners of any ability level; and the AAA at last went along with it. Amateurs and professionals ... Hmmm.

This ruling was the key which began to unlock things. I composed a letter, complete with references to horses and amateurism. (Unfortunately, I cannot now remember the relevant dates, which I provided in the original letter).

"Dear Sir

Now that:

a) Men and women may take part in the same race

b) Amateurs and professionals may take part in the same event (IAAF)

c) Men and *horses* may take part in the same event (Llanwrtyd Wells) all of course under AAA laws, how long do you suppose it will be before the organisers of the London Marathon consider wheelchair users, who clearly qualify under none of the above headings, to be a suitable sub-species to be admitted to their event?

  Yours faithfully

  Tim Marshall

  BSAD National Wheelchair Marathon Co-ordinator"

and sent this to the sports editors of all the "heavy" newspapers: "The Times", "Daily Telegraph" and "The Guardian" for the dailies, and "The Sunday Times", "Sunday Telegraph" and "The Observer" for the Sundays. I sent it on February 18th, sat back and waited. This nasty little missive was intended to make the recipients think, perhaps first of all about the ugliness of the way in which wheelchair users were described, but then, I hoped, about the substantive issue. If the sports editors knew anything about the Great North Run, they might begin to wonder why London hadn't embraced what appeared to be a practice successfully adopted elsewhere. Or they might just be curious about an issue that had provoked such intemperate language. I also sent a copy to Andy Etchells, the editor of "Running" magazine. He had been very supportive in publishing a couple of articles about wheelchair road racing, and so allowing the issue to be aired, and I felt it was worth keeping him in the loop as far as what I was doing.

Before any replies rolled in, there was a Department of Education weekend conference on Physical Education and Recreation for the Handicapped. Liz Dendy had told me about it back in the autumn, so I had applied and was accepted for it. Helpfully, it was held in Birmingham, so it was easy to get to. Most of the content was above me, though I remember thinking that there was a lot being said, a lot of theorising, which seemed to be about what I was actually doing in practice. But rather more important than that was the simple opportunity to meet people, specifically Julia Allton from Tower Hamlets Adult Education Institute, who had organised the "qualifying race" in Docklands just before Christmas, and Margaret Talbot from Trinity and All Saints College in Leeds. With Julia I began discussing how we might develop an effective protest on the day (April 17th); not that I wanted her overt participation in it, because she shouldn't compromise her professional position by getting involved in something which might "attract the attention of the authorities", and because any protest had to be by the athletes themselves, so that we would take the rap for anything that went wrong. Her college was manning one of the feeding stations, so she was thinking of festooning the station with appropriate pro-wheelchair material.

In her professional life Margaret was particularly concerned with inequality in sport and recreation, especially gender inequality. But she was happy to take up the cudgels on this matter, and wrote to Lord Birkett at the GLC, with a copy to Chris Brasher:

> "Dear Lord Birkett
> You will remember that I spoke at the GLC "Sport for All" conference in December on "disadvantaged groups". [*This was the same event where Jenny had met Chris Brasher.*] I write to register my dismay that the GLC has chosen to exclude wheelchair entrants to the London Marathon. Events of this kind offer a rare opportunity for real integrated competition for the disabled, and I am surprised that the GLC has made this decision after the Sport for All conference papers had identified the disabled as a group needing special consideration.
>
> With sensible precautions, elements of safety <u>can</u> be catered for, to allow wheelchair entrants (e.g. the Great North Run): I hope the GLC will reconsider its decision.
> Yours sincerely …"

Just a couple of comments. Although Lord Birkett was in an executive position within the GLC, it won't have been he who took the decision. In any case, it wasn't the GLC who had done the excluding: Illtyd Harrington's last letter made it quite clear that they were not at all happy with the situation. And finally, if the letter ever reached Chris Brasher, it was just another bit of pressure coming from a different angle; all grist to the mill.

Then responses from the newspapers began to come in; firstly the dailies:

The Times: *Dear Mr Marshall,*
Thank you for your letter. I have made our athletics correspondent aware of your thoughts.

The Daily Telegraph: *Dear Sir,*
I fear I cannot tell what flight of fancy will be tried by the organisers of the London Marathon. But as the penny-farthing experiment is not to be continued, I imagine that wheels of any kind would not be acceptable, which seems logical, if not helpful to your cause.

I appear not to have any reply from The Guardian, but this may be attributable to my filing system rather than that they didn't reply.

And then, the Sundays:
From the Sunday Telegraph, nothing at all.

From The Observer (I was surprised to hear from them, because Chris Brasher was their star columnist, and the risk that my letter would be ignored was obvious).

Dear Mr Marshall
Thank you for your letter. I sympathise with your wish to be included officially in the London Marathon, but I fear there is little I can do to help you. On the other hand, I should be glad to have news from you of the national wheelchair marathon when the time comes…

Whilst not practically helpful, this was at least encouraging; but there wasn't actually any progress.

That left The Sunday Times – then seen as a main rival to The Observer in capturing the quality market for Sunday papers; they rang me up. They must have obtained my number either through BSAD or (more likely) through the address from where the letters had been sent. At the time I was still living as an assistant warden in an undergraduate hall of residence, so there was someone in the office during office hours, and they would have given my work number. I was holding a post-graduate tutorial in the department's main meeting room and the phone rang in my office next door. People on legs can accelerate far faster than someone in a wheelchair, so one of the students – Paul, who had written earlier about the validity of his marathon time if there was a parallel wheelchair event – rushed next door, and returned saying "It's The Sunday Times".

" Mr Marshall," they began, "we're ringing about your letter, and wheelchair marathons. Has anyone ever done a marathon in a wheelchair?" What a gift! At that time the fastest wheelchair marathon reported in "Sports 'n Spokes" was 1 hour 48 minutes 9 seconds, by the Canadian Rick Hansen in the 1982 Boston Marathon. There were, of course, several other records of times under two hours, and although, as far as I knew, no one in this country had yet broken three hours, there were plenty of examples of finishing times between three and four hours. I put together an information pack, including the paper from "Sports 'n Spokes" entitled "Sharing the Road", about how successfully to integrate wheelchairs and runners in a single event, and including such copies of correspondence with the organisers of the London Marathon that I'd kept. I also included my letter to John Disley after the 1982 race, along with his intemperate reply (the "perjury" letter). Again, I sat back and waited.

A week later The Sunday Times rang me again.

"We've had an interesting time," they said. "We couldn't contact Chris Brasher – he was in Rome – so we spoke to John Disley instead." A slight pause before they continued: "He's a difficult man, isn't he." I shrugged my shoulders, though there was no one there to see. "I dunno, I've never met him. But I suppose he is, over this business anyway."

They went on to explain how interesting, enlightening even, the paperwork I'd sent them about wheelchair marathons had been, and they hoped to be able to pull it all together for an article in the paper sometime soon. It sounded promising, but then how many more times in the past, stretching all the way back to November 1979, had I been saying that, only to be confounded a few weeks later? So yet again, it was simply a matter of waiting.

Another Enquiry

A few weeks earlier there had been some correspondence with Stoke Mandeville. This is yet another area where the correspondence is incomplete, though enough remains to get the gist of what it was about. I had had no contact with them about wheelchair road racing, not that I had any official position within the organisation itself. But BSAD had recently moved into offices within the Stoke Mandeville complex, and it is inconceivable that BSAD and the British Paraplegic Sports Society – the BPSS – didn't talk to each other. At any event, I had a letter from Joan Scruton, Director/Secretary General of the BPSS, enquiring about wheelchair marathon times in the UK in 1982. I replied, along with information about times in the big American events like Boston and the Orange Bowl. Joan replied on February 8th:

"Dear Tim
Thank you for your letter of 24th January, giving me recorded wheelchair times for marathons in 1982. This is indeed very interesting information and I have passed on copies to Roger Ellis, Chairman of the Track and Field section of the British Paraplegic Sports Society. From the times given, the Americans certainly seem to have the edge on us!
    With kind regards and best wishes
    Yours sincerely ..."

It is worth noting Joan Scruton's position, and the influence it gave her. As Director/Secretary General to the BPSS she was the queen bee of what happened in spinal injury sport in the UK. And she also had a high-up position within the International Stoke Mandeville Wheelchair Games Federation, which gave her a lot of influence internationally too. But both these organisations were about supporting and promoting sport for people with spinal injuries, not sport for wheelchair users. If BPSS or ISMWGF were to get hold of things nationally or internationally, what was going to happen to the non-spinal injury athletes who I was meeting every other week or so on "the circuit"?

Ten days later I had another letter, from Roger Ellis, Chief Remedial Gymnast at the Pinderfields (Wakefield) spinal injury unit:

"Dear Mr Marshall
I recently had a letter from Joan Scruton in which she passed on your comments concerning marathons. As we had only received information about the Orange Bowl marathon in mid- November, we had very little time to make arrangements, therefore we selected the best two performers from the GB athletics squad. We did realise that there were people who had recorded faster times but as you are aware [*I wasn't*] we cancelled due to the absence of funds. We have been instructed by the BPSS to form the Great Britain Paraplegic Athletic Association and intend to hold the inaugural AGM this summer. Once this is formed we would hope to have a marathon sub-committee, perhaps you might be interested in becoming involved in this.
    Yours sincerely ..."

I replied a week later, but don't have a copy.

Two main issues arose from this correspondence. Firstly, if BPSS were to organise a marathon race in this country, in conjunction with a running event, would they allow only spinal injury wheelchair users to take part? And secondly, if BPSS received an invitation to send athletes to an event overseas, would they select (and pay for) only spinal injury cases? Or would they tell non-spinal injury racers too, who might have faster times than spinal injury athletes, but who would need to raise funds from elsewhere? These thoughts were hovering in my mind, but not for long, as London took centre stage once again.

A Last Throw

I'd heard nothing further from The Sunday Times; all had gone quiet. I assumed that their apparent interest had come to naught, and that wheel-chair marathons had somehow slipped off their agenda. This year's race was barely 5 weeks away. If anything was to happen, it had to do so very quickly. As a last, almost desperate, attempt to get the issue in the public eye, I decided to send a letter to: past and present ministers for sport; past and present ministers for the disabled; my MP; and the Lord Mayor of the City of London, through whose fiefdom the marathon wound its way. What I didn't do was include MPs through whose constituencies the marathon went, whether because I didn't think of it or for some other reason I cannot now remember. The letter had to be concise, but take each of the arguments advanced against wheelchair participation and blow it to pieces. So it was going to be longer than I wanted. I sent it from my home address, the flat I'd bought some three years ago and was about to move into full time, and gave myself the semi-official label that Mike O'Flynn had given me long ago.

"Dear …

<u>Wheelchairs and the London Marathon</u>

For the third year running, the organisers of the London Marathon have banned wheelchair athletes from taking part in their event. All represen-tations to them, formal and informal, directly and indirectly, ever since the first event was first announced, have been ignored, or have met with increasingly uncompromising refusals. I am therefore writing to ask for your help in reversing this unnecessary and discriminatory exclusion.

Background

Wheelchair athletes have been competing in running marathons since 1974 in the USA, [*actually, since 1975. This may be a typo, but the difference is hardly material*] and since 1981 in Britain. Over 20 different running marathons in this country have had wheelchair athletes completing the course successfully and safely. The fastest time recorded here is just over 3 hours (though in the USA, sub-2hour wheelchair marathons are common). A formal proposal put in July last year, to stage the British National Wheelchair Marathon in conjunction with the 1983 London Marathon, was turned down flat last month.

The objections

1. Those offered are many and various, and seem to depend on who the organisers talk to. It is against international regulations. People on wheels may not compete against runners, but it is a simple matter to conceive of their competing against each other rather than against the runners, in their own event which happens to be going on simultaneously. It is also against international regulations for men to take part in the same event as women, and for professionals in <u>any</u> sport to take part with amateurs, but the organisers seem to have no difficulty in circumventing <u>these</u> problems.

2 . It is dangerous. An incident on a narrow footbridge in the New York marathon 6 or 7 years ago [*actually, it was 4 years ago*] caused wheelchairs to be banned from that event. There are <u>no</u> similar places anywhere on the London course. [*NB this was not correct, and reflected my ignorance of the course. Just before reaching the Tower, there is a footbridge over the approach to St Katharine's Dock; but by then, about 22 miles into the race, both runners and wheelchairs would be so strung out as to make the likelihood of an accident pretty small.*] All that is necessary is for wheelchair entrants to be identified beforehand, and to be started at the front some five or ten minutes ahead of the runners. This is standard practice in the USA, in many marathons in Britain, and in the Great North Run (Newcastle – South Shields ½ marathon), which last year had 20,000 runners and 61 wheelchairs.

The proposal for the London Marathon this year was for exactly such a structure to the start, and only 20 wheelchairs.

3. It will interfere with the Changing of the Guard. This is one of this year's new excuses. The timing of the event must be such that the guard has changed before the first runners pass [*before they reach The Mall*]. Therefore, it is argued, since the wheelchair entrants might get there ahead of the runners, and contravene the regulations laid upon the organisers, wheelchairs may not be allowed in. This would only be a problem if British wheelchair athletes were recording times in the sub-2¼ hour range. As indicated above, this is not so. In any case, the fact that this is offered as an excuse simply reveals that the organisers have completely ignored the representations made to them over the last 2½ years.

4. There are narrow streets, sharp corners, and cobblestones! The latter are uncomfortable, but hardly a valid reason for exclusion. As to the former, the streets are no narrower and the corners no sharper than on many courses already completed successfully and safely by wheelchair athletes.

5. If it is known that wheelchair athletes are to take part, it will not be possible to attract top-quality overseas runners. Another new excuse this year, and one which makes one wonder who the event is supposed to be for.

Three further points. It is dangerous for wheelchairs to be started at the back [*saying this is a hostage to fortune*] – sometimes thought to be a solution – because wheelchairs tend to be faster than the slower runners, and carving a way through a field of runners is dangerous to Achilles tendons. Runners overtaking wheelchairs (which is what happens when the wheelchairs start first) is, by contrast, an entirely safe situation. Secondly, such is the opposition to the inclusion of wheelchairs that the man [*in a wheelchair*] who took part last year was stated (to me, in writing) by one of the organisers to have committed perjury in completing his entry form. Finally, integrated events such as this offer an all-too-rare opportunity for disabled people to take part fully with able-bodied people, the kind of opportunity which IYDP in 1981 was meant to encourage. It is sad, to say the least, that the organisers of the London Marathon have set themselves against such an opportunity.

I do not know quite what you may be able to do about the matter, other than give it a public airing and maybe to ask some questions in appropriate places, but the BSAD, and I as its "marathon representative" will be grateful for whatever you feel able to do. Many disabled people, not merely those who had hopes of being selected to take part, feel extremely bitter about the policy of the organisers in this respect, the more so since although the event takes place on public roads which are closed for the event, the London Marathon is run by what is essentially a private organisation and no representations can be made via the democratic process to change the policy.

A list of the governors of the marathon is given below; only the Deputy Leader of the GLC is known to be in favour. I do not know to what extent "the organisers" are a different group of people, except that they include Chris Brasher and John Disley, both of whom are opposed.

President, AAA
Chairman, British Amateur Athletic Board
Chairman, Women's Amateur Athletic Association
Chairman, Sports Council
Deputy Leader, GLC [*Illtyd Harrington*]
GLC Director of Arts and Recreation [*Lord Birkett*]
Chairman, London Tourist Board
Representative of Metropolitan Police

I hope to hear from you in due course.
Yours sincerely ..."

I must have been feeling impatient about the apparent non-activity from The Sunday Times about wheelchair marathons: I sent this letter to them on March 5th, a Saturday, but to the MPs and the Lord Mayor not until the following Friday, March 11th. And the Sunday, March 13th, was the day of the inaugural Reading Half-Marathon.

Reading Half-Marathon

A lot of wheelchairs were there, probably around 20 or 25, including many who had taken part in what at the time they had thought was the qualifying event for London nearly three months earlier; I don't remember if Jenny was there, but I think Julia was. The course started at the White Knights area of the university on the south side of the city, went down into and wound around the town centre, including crossing over the river to Caversham, and finished by climbing back up the hill to finish outside the Sports Centre. It being the first event of its kind in the town, there were cameras all over the place. One of them caught me being overtaken by an elderly runner – but he can't have been *that* elderly – climbing up the hill to the finish, and turning around to applaud me as he did so. This photo, published the next day in the local paper, won a prize for best encapsulating the spirit of the occasion. I've no idea what my time was, but I do know I finished second to Mick Karaphillides, one of the London crowd, whom I was to meet on several occasions over the next few years.

So, at what seemed a suitable time after the finish, we started a meeting. Not many had stayed, and those who had were mostly the early finishers and those who had finished high up in the "qualifying race" from Docklands three months earlier. How do you organise a protest? What sort of protest to put on? No one wanted to disrupt the race itself, for although to do so would certainly attract publicity, it would almost certainly be hostile, and as far as possible we wanted people on our side, not against us. For different reasons, there seemed no point in trying to stage something after the last runner had gone. So we tried to concentrate on a "front end" protest, but one which wouldn't disrupt the main race. In the end, the best anyone could come up with was this. We would assemble maybe ½ mile or a mile down the course from the start, and push back as a group along Charlton Way towards the Red start. If/when it looked as though we were going to be blocked from getting any nearer the start, we would turn round and start what would become a truncated race (from our point of view), hoping that we wouldn't be interrupted further down the course, because for "them" to do so would be likely to get fouled up with the main race, absolutely the last thing the organisers would want.

There were several problems with this idea. Clearly, we wouldn't be able to park on the main road used for the race – Charlton Way – so we'd have to use one of the residential roads at right-angles. But wouldn't these be festooned with "No Parking" bollards? It seemed very likely. And how about crash barriers designed to keep the runners and the spectators separate? Again, very likely, but how far along Charlton Way they would have been installed was anyone's guess. So the London lot were left with trying to find out more, though by when was an open question. To judge from later correspondence, Julia was to be the main contact point in London.

Reading was also near where Philip Lewis lived. I don't remember meeting him at the race, either before or after, and the conversation I had with him may have been over the phone a few days later. Whatever form the protest eventually took, it seemed likely that, if it were successful in gaining lots of attention, the police might be involved, and this raised the possibility of a civil or even criminal charge. So I asked Philip if he would be my solicitor if any legal proceedings developed. He said that he wasn't on the active register any longer, and advised strongly against any action that might get us into trouble. So I dropped the matter, hoping that something might turn up which would obviate the need for any protest.

Meanwhile, things were moving on other fronts. The "You can't run against professionals from any sport" business had finally been laid to rest, evidenced by a letter from John Conteh, the boxer, in the "Birmingham Post" on March 9th. He was the team captain of RADAR, a national charity promoting the cause of people with disabilities, and even at this late stage, he was canvassing for runners not yet affiliated to a worthy cause to join the RADAR fundraising team. Presumably, there were other sportsmen and women still canvassing for unattached runners to join their teams.

More importantly, though, my impatience with The Sunday Times had been misplaced. On the same day as the Reading Half-Marathon, their Inside Track column opened with the following:

"No Chairpersons

Contrary to popular belief, the fastest recorded marathon is not Alberto Salazar's 2h 8m in New York in 1981, but Rick Hansen's 1h 48m in Boston a year later – in a wheelchair. In America, wheelchairs are an accepted part of the marathon scene. Over here, despite the fact that they have successfully participated in 20 events, they are seen by the organisers of the London Marathon as a nuisance, and wheelchair athletes are refused admittance. 'We're organising a foot-race, not one on wheels' argues course organiser John Disley, 'and all our talents are going into that. We've already stretched our resources to put on the biggest marathon in the world, and we don't want to jeopardise what we've got.'

Disley's objections to the best 20 wheelchair marathoners competing in conjunction [*with the footrace*] include the possibility of their disturbing the Changing of the Guard (if they arrive too early) or disrupting the opening to tourists of the Tower of London (if they arrive too late). He also cites safety factors: cobblestones, narrow streets, and the necessity of coping with traffic if the wheelchairs are too slow.

All these arguments are dismissed as specious by Tim Marshall, himself a wheelchair Marathoner and a coordinator for the British Sports Association for the Disabled. 'They used to argue that it was against international regulations for wheelchairs to participate. That wasn't true. This year's excuse is the Changing of the Guard.

'None of the problems couldn't easily be overcome. The wheelchair athletes normally start about 10 minutes before the rest, and within a few miles they are spread out over about a hundred yards, so overtaking for the runners is easy. We've coped with traffic and different terrains at all the other marathons we've entered – in fact, none of the others have the roads closed except for the start and finish. And there's no danger of arriving too early because we've not reached the standards of the Americans.'

The last word could well be with the Greater London Council, who sponsor the London Marathon to the tune of £100,000, and provide the course. "You mustn't separate the able from the disabled" says GLC deputy leader Illtyd Harrington, "and we very firmly want these people to enter. The organisers' arguments just do not stand up.""

The race was exactly five weeks away.

Letters began to flow in from MPs. The first arrived from Alf Morris, a well-known campaigner on behalf of disabled people. "I shall be making urgent and personal enquiries to see if there is any way in which I can be of help…" Gary Waller wrote the same day, disagreeing with my basic premise; but at least he had the courtesy to reply. My own MP, Jill Knight, replied the following day saying she didn't really know what she could do, practically, but she would certainly write to the Minister for Sport. And so on. There were eventually replies from Jack Ashley, John Watson, Matthew Paris, Lewis Carter-Jones and Sir Anthony Jolliffe (Lord Mayor of London). A few more trickled in after the race. Much later, I was told that some of the MPs had decided to find out for themselves what the "official" view was, and had trotted across Westminster Bridge to County Hall where the headquarters were. The same person also told me that Brasher and Disley were getting increasingly irritated by having to respond to a succession of MPs pursuing an enquiry which they considered had been put to bed long ago.

Things were on the move in London. Julia wrote to me on March 21st:

"Just a hasty note. Saw your piece in the [*Sunday*] Times – well done. I'm still waiting for map and start details but will send them on as soon as I get them. I understand Geoff Baxter [*I had no idea who he was*] has arranged a half-marathon – believe it to be next week in Romford. So far only 2 places have shown interest in displaying banners and 2 individuals. Rumour hath it the cameras will be on feeding stations on I O Dogs. My contact at that station does not wish to be involved but is chatting up publican and fire station across the road. I'll keep you posted."

It sounded interesting, even if specific details were lacking. But finding out more about the start seemed to be exactly what we were looking for.

Does He Take Sugar?

The BBC had a radio programme "of interest to disabled listeners and their families" which was broadcast on Tuesday evenings. The title came from a well-known cartoon depicting a couple in a café, he in a wheelchair. A waitress stands beside the table and asks the woman "Does he take sugar?" – the implication being that he is not capable of answering the question himself; or that the waitress is uncomfortable about talking directly to a disabled person; or both of these; or any other angle reflecting stereotypical relationships between disabled and able-bodied people.

Some time in the second half of March – after the article had appeared in "The Sunday Times" – I was rung at home and asked if I could go along to the Pebble Mill studios to take part in a discussion on the "Sugar" programme about wheelchairs and marathons, and in particular about the controversy that had recently arisen regarding the London Marathon. I asked if it was going to be live. "Yes," they said. I gulped, and said I would turn up. The programme must have been on either 15th or 22nd March.

At the start of the live interview, they played me a recording of Chris Brasher's criticisms of what I'd been up to, and asked for my response. (Obviously, giving me no advance warning of the questions was the fairest and most objective way of doing things). I went over how it had all started; how far we had got in this country; playing up those races which had welcomed wheelchairs; lauding to the skies the Great North Run (20,000 runners and 61 wheelchairs – no problems); and addressing head-on those problems about London Brasher had raised in his interview. We finished, I think, about five to nine, so there was a bit more of the programme still to go. The studio seemed very happy with proceedings, and there was no re-cap or review to be done, so I went straight home. There, to be greeted by a message asking me to ring Mitch – Ivor Mitchell, the retired special school headmaster who was now a BSAD vice-president.

"You did very well, Tim," he said. "You heard it then?"
"Of course. Didn't they tell you?"
"What? Who?"
"They got on to me through BSAD, and started grilling me about you."
"What?"

"Yes, they wanted to know if you were a madman, a trouble-maker or some-one with a genuine case to make over London. I told them the latter, of course. No, I think you put the case very well. Whether it'll make any differ-ence is another matter altogether, of course, but we can always hope."

On March 22nd The New Statesman, a left-wing weekly journal, published an article about the financial arrangements behind the London Marathon. To say the least it was uncomplimentary, containing as it did suggestions of dodgy deal-ings redounding to the financial benefit of Brasher and Disley. The article was widely reported, but ended up as the subject of a libel suit which, many months down the line, The New Statesman comprehensively lost. Along with all the wheelchair stuff that was beginning to boil up, this article must have been par-ticularly unwelcome as yet something else Brasher and Disley had to deal with.

On Thursday March 24th Jenny sent a long letter to all the people who had been in the Isle of Dogs Half-Marathon. She began thus: "I am writing to explain some of the events which have led up to the unsuccessful attempt to get wheelchair entrants accepted in the London Marathon." She reviewed the chronology of what had gone on, though only as far back as mid-1982, when BSAD first became involved officially. As we have seen, she approached Brasher in person after the GLC sports conference on December 16th, and wrote to him too. Part of his reply, included in Jenny's letter, reads:

"… we are prepared to talk to you about the future – but not until May – but I do urge you to impress upon all your members that they will be putting the event in jeopardy for the future if they try to take part unof-ficially this year." Another offer of jam tomorrow, with a barely veiled threat if anyone tried to barge in this year.

Wolverhampton Marathon

This was held on Sunday 27th March. Since it was local to me, it was easy to trot along on the Saturday to register, using any opportunity to bring up the London issue again. The local paper, the "Express & Star", duly had a picture of me registering, though in the report of my registration there was no mention of London at all; probably, the chance never arose. Unlike afterwards. The course profile was roughly this: a fast start, gradually downhill for 2 miles or so, with the main concern being to avoid hitting manhole covers and patches of repaired road, which, at high speed, might have pitched me out of the chair. The 15 minute headstart was soon swallowed up after the descent finished, because the course turned back on itself with a short, steep climb up Windmill Hill, where the runners caught me up.

The rest of the race became a bit of a blur, though manoeuvring around the roadworks which were the consequence of building a new urban tram system between Wolverhampton and Birmingham was an unusual hazard not met anywhere else. The local paper, though, did the cause proud when reporting on the race. It noted I'd managed a personal best in under 3½ hours, and then: "… he had harsh words for organisers of the London Marathon who have put a total ban on all wheelchair entries in the capital event in three weeks time. And he had pledged to join 30 other wheelchair competitors at the London event to mount a demonstration against the organisers' decision. … Wolverhampton has shown that if a marathon is organised properly there can be room for such entries." And so on.

Breakthrough

Two days later, Tuesday 29th, the following appeared in "The Guardian":

"A certain amount of friction is being engendered in the world of marathon runners over attempts by disabled people to enter and wheel their way around the coming London Marathon.

In the past week Mr Chris Brasher, organiser of the April 7th event [*a mistype – it was on April 17[b]*] has been provoked to fire off a couple of heated letters on the subject. Here is a taster from his letter to the wheelchair-bound Mr Philip Lewis, chairman of the British Sports Association for the Disabled: 'We in this office are getting thoroughly fed up with Mr Tim Marshall (the BSAD negotiator on marathons) who will not accept a straight No, which is given for very good reasons. Instead he is trying to circumvent us by going to the GLC, the newspapers, members of parliament, Uncle Tom Cobley and all. Once upon a time I had a lot of sympathy for the cause of sport for the disabled … but my goodwill is rapidly evaporating.'

Another strong letter went to Mr Alyn Claremont Davies, a 26-year-old former merchant seaman suffering from multiple sclerosis who had entered and proved his fitness with a 22-mile sponsored trip round Deptford. Mr Brasher argues that it would be dangerous for a marathon with more than 10,000 entrants to allow wheelchairs, but he is prepared to consider some arrangement involving later starting times another year. Full discussions with the GLC are taking place today."

There are several points to make here. Firstly, "The Guardian" refers to Philip Lewis as the BSAD Chairman, but the BSAD headed notepaper at this time says it is someone called Colin Bance, of whom I had never heard. I don't know who was what, or when the chairmanship changed from Lewis to Bance (or vice versa), but Brasher brought this up at a press conference 9 days later. Secondly, I was delighted to be upsetting Brasher (and presumably, Disley too). After the initial rejection for the 1981 race, by the simple means of "No reply", and ditto for 1982, the aggressive response by Disley to my post-1982 enquiry (the "perjury" letter), was something I wasn't going to let go.

Thirdly, I suppose my role over the last months had been analogous to that of a lobbyist. So what do lobbyists do, other than approach the press, and MPs, and … Fourthly, I had never heard of Alyn Claremont Davies, though he was apparently well-known in London wheelchair sports circles, and would reappear later on. And finally, yet again we had a reported offer – possibly – of jam tomorrow. But by now, my feeling was that people would find some way of having jam today, perhaps even by trying the sort of protest we had discussed at Reading.

On the Tuesday evening, 29th March, the phone rang at 8.45.

"Hello, Tim Marshall."
"Tim, this is Philip Lewis here. We've had various meetings down here, about the London Marathon as you can imagine. The upshot is that Chris Brasher is going to issue the following press release at 9 o'clock, and I've been asked to clear it with you."
"Why you, Philip, why isn't he on the line?"
"He, er, wouldn't speak to you, and he thought I would be an acceptable intermediary."
"Oh, OK." [*He **must** have been upset*].
"The press release reads like this:

"'Although it is against international regulations for wheelchairs and runners to take part in the same race' [*the bastard, he's twisted things again: same race, no, but same event, yes; and he knows that*], 'in order to allow wheelchair athletes to enjoy the unique experience created by the London Marathon' – [***patronising** bastard! …*] ""

I don't remember the details that followed, but the upshot was that, one way or another, there *was* going to be a wheelchair section in the race. Hooray, at last. But having made my points about the tenor of the press release – if I objected too strongly there might be a risk that the wheelchair section would be aborted – I subsided. Apparently, though, there were still further negotiations to take place, and it didn't look as though I was to be included. I don't remember Philip being clear about what the next steps were, but I could hardly insist on being part of them, for all that my trouble-making had brought us to this stage (for so I thought). The problem was that, not knowing who was in the "negotiating team" I couldn't be sure that whoever was knew enough about wheelchair marathoning to get the best possible deal. All this could hardly be argued out with someone who was merely, in his own words, an intermediary. So the conversation finished, and next morning at work I took the department out for lunchtime drinks, confident that at last we'd managed to get a wheelchair section, but wondering when I would hear anything more.

It didn't take long, though it was in print rather than over the phone. Somehow, probably later than the dateline, but chronologically fitting in here, I had acquired a copy of the "Standard", London's evening paper. In the edition for Wednesday 30th, the following appeared:

"London Marathon runs into trouble

Disabled athletes hoping to take part in next month's London Marathon were at the centre of a bitter dispute today. The Labour-controlled GLC is insisting that wheelchair athletes **WILL** be allowed to compete in the race on April 17th.

But organiser Mr Chris Brasher said today "Wheelchairs will not be allowed in the London Marathon, let's be quite clear about that. It would be far too dangerous."

GLC deputy Labour leader Mr Illtyd Harrington countered firmly "Mr Brasher has got it wrong. Disabled athletes in wheelchairs will be allowed to take part in the race proper and that is that. There is no doubt on that at all." It is thought that about 20 disabled athletes using wheelchairs wish to take part.

Earlier it was understood that the matter had been settled at a midnight meeting at County Hall between the politicians and the race organisers. The hour-long meeting resulted in the following joint statement being issued: 'Discussions have taken place between Mr Tony Banks, chairman of the GLC's arts and recreation committee, Mr Chris Brasher, the race organiser, and Mr Colin Bance, chairman of the British Sports Association for the Disabled, in an effort to resolve the matter of wheelchair athletes. 'The British Sports Association for the Disabled accepts that international rules do not allow people on wheels to take part in running events and that huge marathons such as London, New York and Honolulu could not allow wheelchair athletes to take part because of the danger to other competitors on downhill sections. 'However, in an effort to allow wheelchair athletes to enjoy the unique experience created by the London Marathon, Mr Banks, Mr Bance and Mr Alex Mackay (a GLC councillor) have suggested to the British Sports Association for the Disabled that they appoint an organiser to work with the GLC to ensure that 'wheelers' can share the experience.'

Mr Brasher interpreted this by saying a special race would be organised for the wheelchair athletes *after* the London Marathon had taken place. He criticised GLC councillors. "They are politicians. They are not involved with sports people, whether for the disabled or not. They should stay out of it," he said."

This was not at all promising. What had appeared, a few hours earlier, to be a done deal, although with a few (unspecified) details still to be tidied up, now looked rather less secure. The statement about wheelchairs not taking part with runners, and the assertion of the likelihood of accidents, both seemed to give ground where no concession was needed. Just who was in the BSAD negotiating team? Did they know about Chicago, the Orange Bowl, San Francisco, Berlin, Rotterdam, Paris ... to offer as counter-examples to Honolulu and New York? (And Honolulu was shortly to reverse its decision to exclude wheelchairs, though New York never did.) [*PS: it has now.*]

Furthermore, the quotes attributed to Illtyd Harrington and Chris Brasher seemed to be setting the proverbial irresistible force against an immoveable object. One of them was bound to lose, even if only lose face. Who was more likely to hold sway? Perhaps it was time to contact Julia and the London crowd to see what we could rustle up.

Matters were nudged a little further by an article which appeared the following day, Thursday 31ˢᵗ March, also in the "Standard"; it was evidently keeping a close watch on things:

"Marathon wait for wheelchair men

A decision on whether wheelchair athletes are allowed to compete in the London Marathon is unlikely to be reached before the end of next week – just nine days before the race is due to take place.

Race organiser Mr Chris Brasher said: "We are having talks with the British Sports Association for the Disabled but a report will not be produced before next Thursday. Until then the matter is closed."

The full annual meeting of the GLC's controlling Labour group last night pledged its "100 percent support" to allowing wheelchair athletes to compete, the council's deputy leader, Mr Illtyd Harrington, said today. "There is complete unity at the GLC on this. If the disabled do not take part – then nor do we."

Race organisers say wheelchair athletes cannot compete with runners under international rules – and also fear accidents if they were to be included.

The GLC says it will withdraw its considerable support for the marathon – in which 18,000 runners are due to compete on Sunday April 17ᵗʰ – if they are not allowed. Without GLC support the marathon would be extremely difficult to stage. County Hall provides several hundred helpers on the day, besides much office accommodation, administrative help and reception areas, particularly at the Westminster Bridge race finish. Up to 20 wheelchair athletes want to take part.

Early start

One suggestion being mooted is that wheelchairs should be allowed but with either an early or a late start. Mr Ivor Mitchell, vice-chairman of the BSAD, said members were athletes in their own right and should be allowed in the London Marathon."

Several comments seem in order. Firstly, Brasher seemed to have given a little from the absolutist position he was quoted as taking only the day before. But from my point of view, the same questions which arose during and after the phone call from Philip Lewis seemed to loom just as large, if not larger: who was in the BSAD "negotiating team" and what did they know about wheelchair marathoning?

Set against these concerns was the strong position the GLC had apparently adopted. Allowing a wheelchair section into the race wasn't any longer just the view of Illtyd Harrington, or even Illtyd plus Tony Banks, but that of the whole council – or at least, the majority Labour group. And the article contained a remarkable threat, that of the withdrawal of support for the marathon, together with some hints as to what that might consist of. It wasn't possible to determine whether views expressed in the newspaper were those of the politicians, or whether it was the newspaper itself speculating about what "withdrawal of support" might mean. There was obviously much to be worked through before, according to Brasher, "next Thursday", exactly one week away.

One other comment is worth making here, though it may seem blindingly obvious: "taking part in the London Marathon" for wheelchairs did *not* mean that they would be racing against the runners, but only against each other; they would be taking part *with* the runners, just as men and women run with, rather than against, each other. Astonishingly, this appeared not to be the view of all of what might be called "the opposition".

Jenny Ward, I learned, had been instructed by the BSAD hierarchy to drop all her routine work for the London region and devote herself full time to the business of the marathon. Despite her experience back in December with LBC radio, and the apparent continuing uncertainty about the race

(Brasher's "the matter is closed until next Thursday"), on the same day as the newspaper report, Jenny sent out a letter to all those who had taken part in the Isle of Dogs race, plus anyone else she had heard of who might be interested. It ran thus:

"To Prospective Wheelchair Marathoners

I am sure you will have heard in the media the enormous, if last minute break-through, in allowing wheelchair competitors to compete in the London Marathon.

Yesterday I was asked to be Race Organiser for the wheelchair section. This I am prepared to do but it requires an enormous amount of organisation within the next two weeks if wheelchair competitors are to safely compete in the marathon. I spent the day with the organisers yesterday, working out the safest way that this could take place and I now offer you the chance to participate. If the event is to be safely and efficiently organised in the very short time that's left, I ask that if you enter you accept the arrangements I make are the best possible under the circumstances. [*So it was Jenny who was doing the negotiating. What knowledge did she have of wheelchair marathoning, and what advice was she getting? No criticism of her, chucked into the fray with Brasher and Disley at such short notice. I wasn't, alas, in a position to go down and camp in London for 2½ weeks, even if B&D had been prepared to accept me in a negotiating role.*] Tim Marshall, BSAD Marathon Co-ordinator and the most experienced marathon competitor in this country endorses the arrangements which are being made. [*I don't remember giving any such endorsement, and I have no paperwork to this effect, but as I've said repeatedly the paperwork covering the whole business is often very incomplete. And while it's possible I was the most experienced marathoner in the country, I certainly wouldn't have claimed to be so. It's quite possible that Gerry Kinsella had done more marathons than me, and he certainly had better times.*] This is a fine opportunity to prove that serious wheelchair marathoners can compete alongside runners in a marathon with safety. With the experience gained this year behind us I have the assurance of the Marathon organisers that from the start of the organisation of the 1984 race full participation by wheelchairs will be considered.

B.S.A.D. LONDON MARATHON 1983 – 17th APRIL

1. Up to 20 wheelchair competitors to leave the RED start at GREENWICH at 10 a.m. (this is half an hour after the runners in order that the bulk of the runners will be clear of a hill before the wheelchairs arrive at the hill). [*The hill was the descent down John Wilson Street to the roundabout at the bottom.*]

2. Wheelchair entrants are competing against each other in the race and will be separately numbered.

3. Apart from the two points above wheelchair entrants will have parity with runners, including use of all facilities and eligibility for medals.

[*This was the first point at which a back-end start seems to have been instituted. Would anyone else have been able to achieve a front-end start? To be honest, it's doubtful. Maybe we should have told them to go and talk to Brendan Foster at Newcastle.*]

I am only just beginning on the practical arrangements but I will be grateful if you could confirm below that you would accept the invitation to be a wheelchair entrant. At this stage I enclose some practical details which have been sent to runners, this is in order for you to start to make preparations but not all arrangements apply, particularly in relation to rail transport to the start. It looks as if the most effective way for you to get to the start would be by your own transport with a chauffeur who could then take your transport to the finish. The closing of roads and the enormous amount of traffic will mean a very early assembly at Greenwich and I would be grateful if you would bear this in mind before agreeing to take part. I will be working out the practical details in the next few days but in the meantime I would be grateful if you would indicate by returning the form attached that you are interested in participating in the Marathon event."

Jenny added a hand-written note to me: "Initial first blurb which I will send to anyone you name to me by phone. Much organisation problems re transport etc. but I'm hopeful we can sort it out. Regards, Jenny."

I set about trying to rustle up more punters from the Midlands and the North to put in an entry. All I can recall was the failures. After his initial success in the People's Marathon over two years ago, Mark had found races increasingly hard, and declined. The Southport club had just done a sponsored push, a marathon I think, round an old airfield, and whoever I spoke to declined on behalf of the whole club. That was a pity, because having Gerry Kinsella in the mix would have been a great addition to the occasion, and been an eye-opener for the London lot who, as far as I could tell, never ventured outside London and the South-East. So my efforts to increase participation fell completely flat .Other hospital-based sports clubs in the north showed no interest.

There is another article from "The Sunday Times" about the business. My copy is undated but in the light of its contents it is from April 3rd. Under a banner headline

"Wheelchairs can roll up for the London Marathon"

the article went as follows:

"A selected number of disabled people in wheelchairs is likely to compete with the 17,000-plus runners in the Gillette London Marathon later this month. This is the compromise to be worked out next week after the Greater London Council threatened to withdraw its substantial support because the organisers banned wheelchair athletes.

Ever since some 20 disabled people – including Alyn Claremont-Davies (pictured) – entered the event, which takes place on April 17th, the race director, Christopher Brasher, has been insisting on the enforcement of an International Amateur Athletics Federation rule which defines a marathon as "road *running, walking* and cross-country *running*". [*So he was still refusing to acknowledge that a wheelchair event would be run in parallel with the main running event. Was this a wilful denial of the argument, or did he really believe that the wheelchairs would be competing against the runners?*]

Brasher's main concern is that wheelchairs threaten the safety of other competitors. But disabled entrants, who found themselves barred from the 26-mile circuit through London streets, argue that wheelchair athletes have competed successfully and safely in over 20 different running marathons in Britain... The rift worsened at the end of March with a bad-tempered exchange between Brasher and the disabled people, who were actively lobbying support for their participation. In a letter to the British Sports Association for the Disabled, Brasher said his goodwill towards the disabled was 'rapidly evaporating'.

But the GLC, which does not provide any cash support for the event but provides organisational assistance, entered the controversy last week. A Labour group meeting pledged support for the disabled and said that if wheelchairs were not allowed, the council would withdraw its support.

Yesterday the deputy leader of the GLC, Illtyd Harrington, said that he had talked with Brasher by telephone on Friday and it was clear that there might be a compromise they could work out at a meeting after the Easter weekend. It would probably mean that some wheelchair athletes could participate after vetting for their ability.

Alyn Claremont-Davies, 24 [*NB a previous article had said he was 26*] who has been in a wheelchair for two years, is still training hard on runs between five and 18 miles around his home in Deptford, south London, in the hope that he will be allowed to take part. "I know I can control my wheelchair safely and all I ask is the opportunity to prove myself" he said. Yesterday, both Brasher and his deputy director, John Disley, could not be contacted for comment."

This article was almost exactly halfway between Philip Lewis' phone call to me on Tuesday 29th and the meeting in County Hall on Thursday 7th April.

After all the noise reflected in the articles above, it was hardly to be expected that Brasher would remain silent over the issue; he didn't. The same day, Sunday April 3rd, his article in "The Observer" provided a brief account of recent events – from his point of view, naturally, as this whole book is from mine – and he included remarks such as "emotional blackmail" to describe the kind of pressure that he and John Disley had experienced. This article attracted the attention of George Wilson, the director of RADAR (a national charity promoting the cause of people with disabilities), who wrote to The Observer arguing the case for including a wheelchair section as part of the London event (Brasher had argued for a separate wheelchair event altogether). There followed a short, pugnacious correspondence between the two, ending with a long letter from George Wilson at the end of May, which brought things to a close.

This exchange had scarcely begun when there was then a letter written by Jenny, on April 5th, a Tuesday, to the senior policeman responsible for the overall running of the event from a traffic management perspective. She had already spoken to him by phone, and the letter requested that the first 4½ miles remain closed for half an hour after the starting cannon at 9.30 to accommodate the wheelchair start at 10. This was accompanied by a covering note to Tony Banks expressing disappointment that the wheelchairs were being made to start behind rather than in front, and seeking, if necessary, his support in her approach to the police for the extended road closure. Apparently, there was no problem with this.

Two days later, on Thursday 7th, just ten days before the race, there was a full meeting of all the interested parties at County Hall: Brasher and Disley, Jenny, Lord Birkett, at least one of Banks and Harrington, me, and various others whom I cannot now remember. The meeting was to be followed by a press conference at the Waldorf Hotel in the Aldwych, at which the final outcome of the negotiations was to be announced. I hadn't realised that the event was that close to being cancelled, but it turned out that this was indeed the case.

I went to the meeting with a mixture of trepidation – apart from Brasher's first letter to me back in 1980, all I had ever had from them had been a complete shut-out, with increasing hostility culminating in Disley's "perjury" letter of the previous year, and I wondered what sort of reception I would get from them – and elation, that all the pressurising I had done seemed at last to have borne fruit; with the help of the GLC, of course.

The meeting was held in an upper room of County Hall, overlooking the river and with windows on two sides; very light and airy. Much of the detail of the meeting has been lost – there were no formal minutes, I think – but right from the start there was an assumption that there *would* be a wheelchair section, and what the discussion was about was the fine details. So Illtyd Harrington, not Brasher, had won. There were, however, two matters which produced quite a lot of heat. Firstly, despite the clear statement to the contrary in Jenny's letter that there would be a rear-end start, the matter of a headstart was raised (possibly by me). To John Disley, this was like a red rag to a bull. He was utterly and implacably opposed to a headstart – he threatened to resign his position as race director if a front-end start had been agreed by all the other parties – and all attempts to persuade him otherwise fell on deaf ears. Quite clearly, this point was a deal-breaker, and I didn't have the nerve to hold out for a headstart, at the risk of having the whole race called off.

It seemed to me that there were two arguments which could have been used to support his position. Firstly came the issue of the Changing of the Guard and the closure of The Mall. As I have argued earlier, with the then current state of marathon times in Britain, this wasn't – shouldn't have been – an issue: even with a 10-minute headstart the leading runners would have overtaken all the wheelchairs long before reaching The Mall. But there was no budging either Brasher or Disley. The second argument was much more philosophical, though neither of them used it. Starting the wheelchairs in front might have given them too prominent a role in the overall proceedings, deflecting attention from the primary purpose of showcasing the main race, and in particular the international runners who had been invited to the event.

Neither of these arguments was used. Disley's main argument for not allowing a front-end start was as follows: "If you start the wheelchairs in front and one of them crossed the line first, people would think that he'd won." This argument was reiterated several times. To me, it showed such a staggering naivety as to what "people" might think that it might have been used in a satirical article mocking the whole idea of wheelchairs doing marathons. And it illustrated what to me seemed almost a wilful misunderstanding of the situation: that he seemed to believe the public would think that the wheelchairs would be in direct competition with the runners – against international regulations, of course – and that the public – the spectators – wouldn't understand that there were two races going on (or four, if you count females separately). In no race that I had yet done did spectators ever make such a mis- interpretation, but Disley was deadly serious and I didn't dare call his bluff.

The other item which occasioned if not a shouting match then a lot of unproductive heat, looked back to a piece in Jenny's letter of March 31st, about our having equal status regarding use of feeding stations, medals etc. Brasher was as adamant as Disley had been over the front-end start that we couldn't have London Marathon medals. We wouldn't be doing the London Marathon, since this was a foot-race, and medals were awarded to those who had completed the foot-race, not to those who had traversed the distance, and route, in a wheelchair. There was an agitated discussion about how to create a medal with an appropriate design; some decision was eventually reached, not the least bit satisfactory to either Jenny or me, but again we were stuck against the hard-line position taken by Brasher.

We also had to accept, not just a rear-end start half an hour behind the running start, but also a "guide car" that would travel slowly in front of the wheelchairs until we had reached the bottom of John Wilson Street and turned left towards Greenwich. This would have been a very fast section of the course – as future years proved – and it was felt necessary to protect the last runners from wheelchairs which might have been travelling at well over 20 mph approaching the bottom of John Wilson Street.

So we trooped across Westminster Bridge to the Waldorf. I don't think I'd realised before the County Hall meeting how close to a complete cancellation of the whole event we had come, with on the one hand the GLC's threat to "withdraw co-operation" from the race, and on the other, Disley's threat to resign as race director if we/the GLC had insisted on a front -end start. There was a brief introduction by Illtyd Harrington mentioning that discussions had taken place between the three parties: London Marathon Promotions, the GLC, and BSAD. There wasn't a hint of the rancour that had filled the newspaper columns for the last several weeks before he handed proceedings over to Chris Brasher.

His opening words were "The London Marathon scheduled for April 17ᵗʰ will take place" as though to assuage doubts which might reasonably have arisen in anyone following recent press reports. There was almost an audible, collective sigh of relief from the audience, even if cancelling the event would, in the short term at least, have made a far bigger, and more interesting, story. Brasher went on to explain revised arrangements for the race, including that there would be a rear-end start for the wheelchairs, before handing over to the audience for questions.

I hadn't a clue who was in the audience – by name, that is, I just assumed that they were sports reporters from newspapers, TV and radio; but I do remember the first question from the floor. "Pat Butcher, athletics correspondent for The Times. Isn't a rear-end start for the wheelchairs dangerous?" The question was referred to me. I gulped – should have seen this coming. Over the last few years I had written several articles about wheelchair road racing, including two or three in what had come to be the most popular magazine on road running in general, "Running". I felt the editor, Andy Etchells, had been generous towards the issue of wheelchair participation in road running events. But my articles had frequently included a statement to the effect that rear-end starts were dangerous to runners. Was Andy in the audience, and ready to quote my own words back at me? And did Pat Butcher have any of those articles at his fingertips, ready to do the same?

I made some anodyne comments about preferring a front-end start, but without going as far as saying that it hadn't been possible to agree on this – that much must have been obvious to anyone who knew anything about the subject – and then remarked on the ability of wheelchair athletes to control their chairs in a crowd. Astonishingly, no one picked the point up, and the discussion moved elsewhere, with the whole conference being over in an unconscionably short space of time (I don't even remember whether there were drinks and nibbles at the end, but I think not). At the end, I went to talk to Jenny, who had to sort out final details over the next ten days with the GLC, Brasher and Disley, the police and, of course, the runners themselves. And then I started back up to Euston, finding myself in the company of both John Walker (the People's Marathon) and Billy Wilson (the Wolverhampton Marathon). To them, the whole business seemed like a storm in a teacup, or something out of "Alice in Wonderland": a great hoo-ha about nothing.

What eventually emerged from Jenny's work was that we would have to find our own way to the start on Charlton Way, and make our own arrangements to be collected at the end and returned to our vehicles. Race numbers would be issued at the start, and we had strict instructions to stay behind the pace car right to the roundabout at the bottom of John Wilson Street.

I spent the afternoon and early evening of April 16th over at the house of some friends in south-west London, before driving over to the start and parking on a dead-end piece of tarmac somewhere on the Blackheath to spend the night in the van. It wasn't quite as simple as that, however, because I'd spent the money the BBC gave me for appearing in "We are the Champions" on buying 25 T-shirts with the slogan "LONDON BANS WHEELCHAIRS" on the front. They were to be used if the planned protest ever got off the ground, so I had spent the Saturday afternoon painting out "BANS" and painting in "WELCOMES", hanging them on the washing line to dry. But the Sunday morning, with everyone milling around at the start, was no time to try to get rid of them, and I ended up leaving a large bag with one of the helpers to distribute as they saw fit.

Many of those at the start I already knew, either from other races or because they'd written to me or phoned me over the previous months. Most prominently, Alan Robinson, who had won the first two Great North Runs was there – I saw him as a likely winner – and though Gerry Kinsella had reappeared on the official entry list, he wasn't actually there – pity, I thought. Nor, surprisingly, was Mick Karaphillides, who had won the Reading Half Marathon only a few weeks before. And then there was an older man, maybe in his mid–late 50s, who said he was William Charlton, who wasn't on Jenny's official start list, but seemed genuine enough, so he was issued with a spare number. We'll meet him again in 1984.

One other feature of note: recognising the potential hazards of a rear-end start for runners, many of the entrants had furnished themselves with audible signals to indicate that a wheelchair was coming through: either a bicycle bell or (louder) a whistle or (loudest of all) a sailing fog-horn. There were no central instructions about this, it just seemed a sensible thing to do. Amidst the melee I managed to find Ivor (climbing club again) and gave him the van keys to drive the van to Waterloo.

The best way of describing what happened is to quote the article I wrote for "Sports 'n Spokes":

"GILLETTE LONDON MARATHON 1983

Two and a half years of letter-writing, argument, persuasion, pointing to examples everywhere else in the country, approaches through the recreation department of the city council, none of this cut any ice with the organisers who persisted, for the third year running, in refusing to allow a wheelchair section in "their" race. Then, five weeks before the race, the national press became interested. One of the organisers writes a weekly column, and his newspaper's main rival was obviously delighted to indulge in a bit of journalistic side-swiping; it must also have seemed a good story. The city council took up the issue again and threatened to withdraw their facilities – the roads!! – [NB see p.158] if wheelchairs weren't allowed in. Hurriedly-called late-night meetings in London, press statements … Suddenly, the issue became one for national discussion, in all the newspapers (complete with cartoons) on national radio and television – all the media got in on the act as the race approached.

A messy compromise, fully satisfactory for none of the parties involved. The organisers didn't want us there at all. The city council wanted the wheelies to be fully part of the race, the organisers and the (running) athletics authorities refused, saying we couldn't be part of the running race, but could have our own, separate race ("The Gillette Wheelchair London Marathon" – what's in a name? – we weren't really bothered). We wanted, argued, pleaded to be allowed to start in front; the organisers and the athletics authorities refused, and we didn't feel strong enough to call their bluff over an implied threat to withdraw recognition from the event (thus disestablishing both the men's and women's national championships, and depriving dozens of runners of official qualifying times for the world championships in Helsinki in August – who wants that kind of responsibility?)

Ever tried to organise a wheelchair marathon at 10 days notice (all that was left after the final rounds of negotiation)? No qualifying times, just who do you know who you think will do well? Several invitees declined, either because they hadn't had the time to train, or because they disagreed with the rear-end start (so did we – but that or nothing: what would you choose?). Nineteen confirmed starters.

The day before the race was beautifully warm, 65–70 degrees, with a gentle breeze; but the forecast was lousy – and right. 45–50 degrees the next morning, with intermittent heavy rain throughout the race. We had to start 10 minutes after the runners from the "Red" start (there are two starts in the London race, with the routes converging after 4 miles), and until we met the "Blue" start we had to keep behind an official car. The gently undulating beginning, and the 135 feet descent in ¾ mile from 2½ miles out, were totally wasted for the chairs, as the first 4 miles took 35 minutes, whereas we reckoned we could have done it in under 15.

Then came the problem of trying to weave through the ankles of the 19,000-odd runners without hitting them. Some of us had aerosol canister foghorns; they helped, but were not a solution. For the first time in 7 marathons and 2 half marathons the writer heard complaints from runners about the presence of wheelchairs: the way that we were coming across them, from behind, you can't really blame them; but the blame really belonged elsewhere.

The course is an historical one, beginning on the line dividing eastern and western hemispheres (the Greenwich Meridian), moving into the eastern hemisphere until reaching the river, turning back westwards through dockland, over Tower Bridge and then back to the east, returning westwards again through the grounds of the Tower of London and on alongside the river, with a finish connecting Trafalgar Square, Buckingham Palace, the Houses of Parliament and Westminster Bridge. Surfaces variable: they include approximately 1 continuous mile of cobblestones before, during and after the Tower; but at their best they are superb.

Once released from behind the official car the race began in earnest. Perry, Fletcher, Marshall and Dobson made an early collective break, and were never seen again by the rest (once you make a break through a crowd of runners it becomes very difficult for the following chairs to move through – you can't even see who you're chasing, have no idea how far ahead they might be, and the psychological barrier is big). The first three alternated the lead until mile 10 when Marshall was left by the others. They kept more or less together round the lonely Isle of Dogs (more dockland), but Perry made his break at about 20 miles and was clean away. Fletcher subsequently broke Dobson about 2 miles later, and Marshall took Dobson back with two miles to go.

The times are pathetically slow by world standards, though we reckon that perhaps 40 minutes of this was due to the starting arrangements. We were all adamant that we should have started in front, and this notion seems at last to be getting through to lots of people in and around the running scene (though not, alas, the organisers or the Amateur Athletic Association). I estimate we're 5–6 years behind the USA in our performances, for the fastest time yet set in Britain remains Kinsella's 3 hours 1 minute in the Mersey Marathon. Things may yet change: if he's fit, some of us will be meeting George Murray in the British American marathon in May, and the Scots are hoping to tempt over another North American star for their race in the fall.

Results:

1	Gordon Perry	3h 20m 07s	10	Denise Smith	4.29.03
2	Joe Fletcher	3.25.03	11	Graham Young	4.35.11
3	Tim Marshall	3.26.15	12	Andy D'Costa	4.44.10
4	Leroy Dobson	3.27.40	13	Alyn Claremont-Davies	4.52.44
5	Charles Raymond			3.52.55	14
	Chaz Sadler	5.01.35			
6	Ernie Gomec	3.55.50	15	Rick Cassell	5.11.38
7	James Gilham	3.56.57	16	Rudi de Christopher	5.56.19
8	Sha Estandfari	4.08.16	17	Jo Roberts	6.09.03
9	Stuart Anderson	4.29.03			

Sports 'n Spokes did publish it, under the title "Marathon Mix-up" – abbreviated to about 100 words, but without the results! I guess they found the times embarrassing.

There are a few points to make. Firstly, the cobbles in the Tower were just as bad as we had been warned about. You couldn't keep any momentum going, and in effect this meant that each one could only be tackled with a separate push – very dispiriting. Even worse, they led up to a climb out of the Tower through Traitor's Gate – but although the surface here was smooth, you had no momentum with which to launch into the climb, so you had to do it from a standing start – again, very discouraging. From then on, however, the surfaces were superb, especially along The Mall, and turning into Birdcage Walk and along Great George Street, you could see Big Ben and Parliament Square, beyond which was the finish. But the finish: past Parliament Square was Westminster Bridge, on the far side of which was the tape. To get up there was a climb, not very long and not very steep, but rising gently for perhaps 20 feet to the crest of the bridge before falling slightly for the last 20 yards or so. After 26 miles, that climb seemed a cruel way to end it all.

And then, as I reached the finishing line, there was Alan Robinson, winner of the first two Great North Runs – what was he doing here, surely I wasn't 4th, when had he come past? He told me not to worry, he hadn't completed the race, but had been swept up – when and where I never discovered – and transported to the finish. Of William Charlton there was no sign, but along with Alan and the 17 confirmed finishers he presumably made the 19th starter.

Truth Will Out

Sitting on the terrace outside County Hall, I was thinking of trying to find Ivor, who had driven the van from Greenwich to Waterloo. But Illtyd Harrington turned up. "Hello, Tim," he said, "I want you to come and meet some people." As we left the terrace he commiserated with me at finishing only third, but said that there had been a presentation to Gordon by Ken (Livingstone) – I forgot to enquire as to whether Denise, who had won the women's race, was similarly honoured. But what came next was an astonishing revelation about what had happened in the weeks between my letter to the politicians and Philip Lewis' telephone call.

The story unfolded as we entered what seemed like the dungeons of County Hall. What comes next is my memory of the conversation. It is reported as such, and though it can't be a strictly verbatim record of what he said, it is as close to the truth as I can remember; and the gist of it is absolutely and completely true.

"I expect you're wondering how all this came about," he said. I had fondly imagined that all the pressure I been putting on had eventually resulted in Brasher and Disley conceding, and said as much; but no, they had resisted all the pressure resulting from my letters to past and present ministers for sport, and ditto disability. "Oh no," he said, "there was lots more water under the bridge yet. You know The Sunday Times went to talk to Brasher and Disley?" "Well, Disley, actually, Chris Brasher was in Rome. That resulted in the article in the paper in March."
"Yes, That's right. But they were so astonished at Disley's vitriolic response to their approach that they thought there must be something more to dig into. You know what the Sunday papers are like."
"Yes."

"Well, they went to the IAAF in Richmond and asked them what was their position regarding the participation of wheelchairs in road races. The IAAF said it was nothing to do with them, as they weren't the governing body for wheelchair racing. 'Of course,' they continued, 'you can't have the wheelchairs competing directly against the runners, as far as we are concerned that would be illegal, and we would de-recognise the running race and any results that came from it.' The Sunday Times persisted. 'But if the wheelchair race were run *in parallel* with the running race, that would be OK would it, not a problem?' 'Not for us it wouldn't be. Of course, there might be issues of safety, but that's a matter for the race organisers, not for us.'"

(I never found out exactly what The Sunday Times managed to extract from the IAAF over its position on wheelchairs and road racing, but in the light of what followed it seems unlikely to have been just a verbal statement of their position. I can only imagine that it was a simple written statement clarifying the issues set out above: that they were not in any sense a governing body for wheelchair racing; that wheelchairs could not be described as racing against runners in a road race (and that to do so would invalidate any and all running results from such a race); but that there were no laws or IAAF rules or regulations forbidding the staging of a wheelchair race being run in parallel with a foot-race; and that organisers may need to pay particular attention to safety issues should they decide to run such a parallel event.)

"What happened next," Illtyd continued, "is that The Sunday Times came to us, armed with this information from the IAAF. As you can imagine, we found this very interesting indeed – we were sympathetic to your cause almost right from the start, but had been completely stymied by the 'against international regulations' argument. So we took what the paper had just told us – given to us – and asked Brasher and Disley to come and see us."

(I don't know whether this meeting was one of the routine meetings which were no doubt a regular feature of the run-up to the whole event, or whether it was a special, one-off meeting; nor do I know exactly when it took place, though it must have been within a very few days before, or even the same day as, Philip Lewis's phone call to me. At any event, there was a meeting, at which the GLC, in the shape of Harrington and Banks, re-introduced the subject of a wheelchair section.) "'Not this one again' Brasher and Disley said. 'We've already explained that it's against international regulations; why can't you accept this?'

"'Are you sure of that?'

"'Absolutely.'

"'Well, this is what your own international governing body says.'

"At this point we showed them the statement that the IAAF had given to The Sunday Times, and which they had passed on to us. As you can imagine, they (Brasher and Disley) weren't very happy; but for them, things were about to get worse. We'd prepared very carefully for this meeting – we are politicians, you know."

We had reached a lift, but before calling it he carried on with the story.

"So we pressed home the point. 'You told us it was against international regulations to have wheelchairs and runners taking part in the same event. For months, you have peddled this line to us, and we believed you. Now, it appears that there are no such regulations forbidding the parallel running of such an event, and your own international governing body says so.' A pause. 'What you told us wasn't true.'" [*Ouch!*] Brasher and Disley must have been feeling pretty uncomfortable by now, but the next move made things a lot worse for them.

"'What else have you told us that isn't true?'"

[What a devastating question – what could anyone have said in response? The *coup de grace* followed.]

"'We think the marathon has been an excellent development for London, for the people who live here, in fact for the whole country. We want to enhance the event with the inclusion of a wheelchair section. We all know that, under IAAF laws, and despite what you told us, this is not forbidden. If you persist in refusing to allow a wheelchair section in this year's race, we may have to reconsider our application to the police to have the roads closed for the event'."

In chess, this is known as *zug-zwang* (literally, "train crash"). It's your move, you *have* to move a piece, move *any* piece *somewhere*; but anything you do will, in your own eyes, make things worse than they already are. It was this meeting, and Brasher and Disley's response to the GLC, that resulted in Philip Lewis' phone call to me on that Tuesday evening.

The room upstairs was full of the great and the good, all seemingly involved with the marathon specifically or athletics and sport in general. Illtyd introduced me to Roger Bannister, but our conversation was somewhat desultory before he was taken away by someone else. After about half an hour I left, and found Ivor outside, waiting patiently for me to turn up. He was beaming, thought the whole thing was marvellous, the little man had prevailed over the big man, and all was well with the world. I didn't even think to ask him into a café for a drink before taking the keys and driving back to Birmingham.

The question remained: why were Brasher and Disley so deeply opposed to the existence of a wheelchair section in the first place? I never found out, so what follows is inevitably speculation. Firstly, and probably most important, London was modelled on the New York Marathon organised by Fred le Bow, who banned wheelchairs. Why, I don't know, but it's easy to imagine that he advised against the inclusion of a wheelchair section for whatever reasons *he* had (a nuisance, too much trouble, dangerous to runners, wheels are not the same as legs, against international regulations ...). Secondly, London was, and is, a foot-race; people on wheels are different, and therefore not eligible to take part. This view is at least consistent with Disley's view of how the public would view matters "... if a wheelchair crossed the line first, people would think that he'd won." Personally, I would credit the watching public with more sense than that.

One of the consequences of the "foot-race" argument is, of course, that wheelchairs cannot take part in "The London Marathon", and therefore, even if they trundle along the same course as the runners at roughly the same time, they will not be eligible to receive a London Marathon medal, which is for runners only. To describe this attitude as mean-spirited would be overly generous to Brasher, who, fortunately, changed his mind the following year. Lastly, comes the "against international regulations" argument, which is valid only if organisers think that runners and wheelchairs are competing directly against each other; this is simply a restatement of the earlier position, and I would guess that most (all?) don't think that at all.

Aftermath

As may be imagined, many things flowed from the events described above. In the week following the race, Jenny sent me a long letter, the first page of which I have lost, but the second page reads, tantalisingly, as follows:

"... could also be helpful in preventing a resurrection of the political saga revolving around Alyn Claremont-Davies. I feel this is going to be the first question he and his M.P. ask when they hear about next year's Marathon. If we're freed of this stupidity we will all have more time to concentrate on the important aspects of safety in the race. No answer expected but I thought it would be helpful for you to have these points to think on before our next meeting. I enclose a copy of Alyn Claremont-Davies's letter and my reply."

This looked ominous. What was the issue that might occasion him bringing in his M.P.? The name was familiar from the newspaper articles, but he hadn't been at the April 7th meeting in County Hall, and I hadn't been introduced to him at the start, so who was he, and what was he upset about? The letter didn't really clarify anything at all. Here it is:

"Dear Jenny
I was rather disappointed after Sunday's marathon event about a couple of points

1.   I was told by you that the medals that the wheelchair entrants received on finishing would be the same as those received by 'able-bodied' competitors. My medal, for one, was different to those given to 'able-bodied' people which rather spoiled the feeling of the day for me. My medal did not include any people, running, walking, or in

wheelchairs on Tower Bridge so I feel that it is only a souvenir of London and not of the London wheelchair marathon.

2.   I and many other, unrelated, people feel that my efforts and publicity to get wheelchairs accepted in THE London marathon has gone totally unrecognised by the BSAD and the commentator on BBC television.

3.   As the GLC were totally behind having wheelchairs participating in THE London marathon I cannot understand why you agreed with Mr Brasher to have a separate event, that could easily have been part of the london marathon, was decided on. With the GLC being behind me this year wheelchairs could have participated in THE London marathon this year and not at some time in the future or at a never never date.

4.   I thought that out of courtesy I would have been told about the meetings that were being arranged between you and Mr Brasher, or invited to the meetings even if you decided to take someone else to speak.

I am sorry if I sound rather bitter about the course of events but I feel that without my effort wheelchairs would not have run on Sunday at all and if BSAD had been a little more organised and working for disabled people wheelchairs would have been in THE LONDON MARATHON 1983 and not a second class race.

    Yours sincerely

    Alyn Claremont-Davies"

I found most of this letter baffling: what did he mean by THE London Marathon? In principle, there are three ways of starting a wheelchair section: at the front, with or without a headstart; at the back, with a defined lag after the start, hopefully as soon as possible after the last runners have started; or scattered throughout the assembled runners at the start, in accordance with their estimated finishing times, as had originally been proposed for the Great North Run. Which of these arrangements did he think would have constituted THE London marathon? It was as clear as mud. And whilst his comment about the medals was fully justified, he evidently knew nothing of the knife-edge we had reached on April 7th. As for the comments about getting greater coverage of the wheelchair race from the BBC, who *wouldn't* have wanted greater coverage?

He evidently had some standing in London regarding disability sport, for he had been quoted in one of the newspaper articles, and he also referred to his meeting(s?) with the GLC. But I had met the GLC several times and his name had never been mentioned. (Two things happened for 1984: it was accepted by Brasher and Disley that the wheelchair finishers would receive a full, London Marathon medal. What would have happened if news of the ban in 1983 had received wide public attention is a matter of speculation, though I don't think Brasher and Disley would have come out of it smelling of roses. And, recognising the injustice of the 1983 decision, the GLC put on a reception in 1984 at which the 1983 finishers were finally awarded full 1983 medals.)

Jenny's reply – stressing the short time there had been to organise the wheelchair section, and the difficulties which had had to be circumvented – must have acted as a safety valve, for to the best of my knowledge there was no further approach from A C-D, nor his MP.

Comments from other participants were rather more enthusiastic. From Graham Young, for example:

"Dear Jenny,
Many thanks for the results, and thank you for putting in all the hard work at the last minute to make this event possible on the day. The organisation was first class and I only see one problem, that must be worked out before 1984. As you know from the beginning, we would have a problem with the start because of starting from the back.

Problems that this caused were:-

1. More danger to the runners on foot because of the need to pass on route
2. Wheelchairs covering a larger distance because of going round runners
3. Slowing down wheelchair times

I suggest the wheelchairs start from the front 15 minutes before the main start. This will allow the wheelchairs to clear the fastest section before the first runners come by. It is also much easier for runners to pass a single wheelchair on route rather than the other way round.

Looking at the times that were made by the wheelchairs I can see the leading wheelchairs finishing in 1984 in 2 hours 30 minutes allowing for an open road, better wheelchairs, fitter competitors, and better under-standing of the race. With this in mind very few runners will be meeting the wheelchairs at all.

I hope this has been of some help, and I am looking forward to another great marathon in London in 1984.
Best wishes
Graham Young
P.S. The public reaction has been fantastic. My phone never stopped for two days and people have also written letters to myself and Olive. I think this speaks for itself."

There were letters, too, from helpers – unofficial stewards whom Jenny had persuaded into standing by at places on the course potentially difficult for wheelchairs: the Cutty Sark, St Katharine's Dock (a narrow footbridge) and the Tower of London. None of them reported needing to assist any of the chairs, though the steward at the dock reported a slight slowing down of the wheelchairs at the entrance to the Dutch Bridge as runners and wheelchairs filtered together, rather like traffic merging where two roads join.

This was all very gratifying, but the crunch would come when Brasher and Disley turned up with comments from the runners. Another letter from Jenny at the end of the month brought news of contact from Alison Turnbull, the deputy editor of "Running" magazine, who wanted a results list – all the timing of the wheelchair race had had to be done by BSAD stewards quite independently of the timing of the main race, from which there was no support for wheelchair timing at all, and who said that she was pursuing rumours about two alleged incidents involving a wheelchair and runners. Between them they agreed that nothing would go into print until facts about the incidents were clearly established.

I have no further information about this line of enquiry, but the accident issue was brought fully into the open at a meeting on June 1st between Brasher and Disley on the one hand and a contingent from BSAD on the other, which included Jenny and Graham Young (writer of the sensible letter above) and the new BSAD chairman, Colin Bance (who had been at the April 7th meeting in County Hall and the subsequent press conference at the Waldorf Hotel, the first time I had met him). Brasher read out about 14 letters from runners, three of which reported injuries. Potentially this was very serious, though entirely attributable to the rear-end start. Largely these were just bumps and bruises, and though there was one who had Achilles tendon damage, it responded to treatment. The most disturbing incident occurred on the Isle of Dogs, where a wheelchair competitor ignored a marshal who told him to stay on one side of the road as traffic flowed normally on the other. He knocked the marshal over and collided with a lamp post. I don't know if we ever found out who the individual was – had we done so he would have been barred from the race in future.

The other matter which occasioned many complaints was, predictably, the bells, hooters and whistles which the wheelchairs had used to warn runners of their approach, entirely the consequence of the rear-end start. Clearly, the accidents and the audible warnings could be avoided completely by a head-start. Interestingly, at the meeting, Brasher and Disley insisted on a code of conduct for wheelchair participants in future – thus acceding to the idea that there would indeed be a wheelchair section next year – and seemed to have accepted the idea of a front-end start as the way to organise things. In practice, the front-end start almost entirely obviated the need for a code of practice at all, but here it is. Some of these points were almost certainly adopted directly from the rules laid down by Stoke Mandeville for racing wheelchairs used in the various spinal injury games:

"1.   WHEELCHAIRS
a) Must be mechanically safe and sound
b) Should be clear of any protrusions – particularly at the side which could endanger runners
c) The wheelchair shall have two wheels for propulsion and at least one for steering

d) The maximum diameter of the inflated drive wheels shall be 70 cms

e) The philosophy that the wheels are driven directly by the hands without the aid or use of gears, chain levers or other mechanical devices will be maintained. [*NB this looked backwards to a few years earlier when someone had turned up at Boston with a mechanically-driven, fully geared, machine, rather like a Meccano-built version of the Cyclops hand-bike I had seen in Denver in 1978; he wasn't allowed to start, but this kind of equipment eventually gave rise to the sport of Handcycling.*] The drive wheels shall have one hand-rim of any diameter solidly attached to each using any method not constituting a hazard to any other competitor. Hand rims may have coatings to facilitate good grip. When foot supports are used provision must be made to prevent the feet from sliding from the foot supports.

2. Klaxons will not be carried or used.
3. A wheelchair competitor may not demand right of way.
4. Directions given by race officials and marshals must be obeyed."

What would be fascinating to know would be the comments Brasher and Disley had received about the wheelchair section in that first race. It is inconceivable that they had no comments from race organisers elsewhere in Britain, or indeed further afield, but, unsurprisingly, we were not privy to any of them.

1984 And Beyond

The group brought together by Jenny in the last few weeks couldn't continue in such an *ad hoc* fashion; something more formal was needed. Jenny herself was leaving, going to teach PE and Games in a girls' finishing school in Switzerland. From nowhere, it seemed – that is to say, I can't remember how it came about – Alan Crouse popped up. He had first appeared some time after Philip Lewis' phone call to me on March 29th. One meeting was held in his house between the press conference at the Waldorf and race day itself, and two or three meetings were held at his home shortly after the race. With Jenny's imminent departure we needed someone to chair the group who had the necessary time and skills to guide the development of the wheelchair section over the next few years. None of the racers felt able to take on this role, BSAD couldn't offer anyone, so Alan it was. As head of the British arm of a major office supplies and equipment company, he presumably had greater flexibility over the availability of his time. For the next few years meetings were held in Islington Town Hall at 7.30 in the evenings – not the easiest of times for someone who had to get back to Birmingham the same evening.

There had been such a stir in the three weeks leading up to the race that there was bound to be interest in the future. Unexpectedly, one of the early enquiries came from abroad. I was rung up by Carol Hayes of the Irish Wheelchair Association asking if we were willing to open up the race to her athletes, how did it work and what were the conditions? That was easy to deal with: the committee agreed immediately to the internationalisation of the event in this way, and so the Irish turned up in 1984 with three athletes: Kevin Breen, Jerry O'Rourke and Kay McShane.

In discussions with Brasher and Disley there was at this stage apparently no problem with a front-end start becoming mixed up with the Changing of the Guard on The Mall. They must have recognised that the current times posed no immediate threat to that hallowed event; the timing issue was to arise later. But after all the hoo-ha about the race, I was asked to give a talk to the annual meeting of the Spinal Injuries Association in September. Afterwards, I was approached by Rosalie Wilkins (later to become Baroness Rosalie Wilkins), who was the chief presenter of Central TV's "Link" programme "of particular interest to disabled viewers and their families". It had been, she thought, quite a strong story with me, it seemed, at the centre. They (Link) were thinking of making some half-hour programmes about individuals living within the Central coverage region, and would I consider being one of these? So I came to have a half-hour TV programme all about me, and the issues which the struggle for the marathon had evoked. Their idea was that the programme would culminate with the 1984 race, at which I confidently expected to break 3 hours. Filming went on during early 1984, including film of me teaching my post-graduate students as well as sailing (in a Wayfarer, not in the trimaran) and some shots taken the day before the race in my new racing wheelchair in the Docklands.

As part of the filming I went to the pre-race Pasta Party at the Royal Lancaster Hotel. Madge Sharples, the elderly Scottish runner, was there, as was Ron Pickering, interviewing whoever might be found – amongst them, William Charlton. He had begun to be seen at a number of races around the country, usually rattling a collection box labelled BSAD, though no one in the organisation knew anything about him. Ron Pickering later reported that he'd met "a smashing man who had done as many as 512 marathons, *and* the Pennine Way, all in his wheelchair!" I wrote to Ron afterwards pointing out the absurdity of what he'd been told, but never had a reply.

And so to the race. William Charlton was there (of course!), but he wasn't allowed to start. Later that year he was picked up by the police at the finish of the Robin Hood (Half-?) Marathon with a very full collection box. It transpired that he'd appeared at many races during the year, always under the same guise, with neither BSAD, nor any other charity as far as could be ascertained, receiving any money from his activities. What happened to him, I don't know.

For me, the race was a disaster, the more so because I'd given the TV people estimates of my times at particular points on the course, based on a finishing time of 2 hours 50 minutes. Right at the start, pushing along Charlton Way, it became obvious that I hadn't set the wheelchair up correctly: I hadn't strapped my knees together to give a "platform" to rest my trunk against, and instead, when leaning forwards, my knees parted and my trunk fell forwards and downwards, putting huge pressure onto the front wheels and slowing me down so much that I was 8 minutes slower than in 1983 in what was supposed to be a bespoke racing chair. A consultation with my wheelchair designer/manufacturer, and a simple adjustment to the chair, resulted only 6 weeks later in completing the Piccadilly Marathon in 2h 47m 32s, over ¾ hour faster than my London time, and within 10 minutes of Kevin Breen's winning time at London of 2h 38m 40s – though, naturally, courses are very different, and the Piccadilly course was, I thought, possibly faster than London, for a wheelchair at least.

On the few occasions subsequently that I met Brasher and Disley there still seemed to be a simmering resentment that they had been trumped over the wheelchair issue. But Brasher at least seemed to acknowledge that wheelchair marathoning could be an exciting event to watch: in the 1985 race, Jerry O'Rourke towed Chris Hallam all the way round the course until, as they crossed Parliament Square and reached the slight rise of Westminster Bridge, Hallam put in a tremendous sprint to overtake O'Rourke on the crest of the bridge. Brasher roared on the fiercely competitive finish, much as he roared on Ingrid Kristensen when she was trying to break 2 hours 20 minutes in what would then have been a world's fastest time for a female runner (she didn't make it). And at the end of the 1985 television transmissions, the BBC showed a final panel with mug shots of three winners: man, woman, and wheelchair.

Kevin's time, the front-end start and the improvements in wheelchair design presaged a forthcoming clash between the start time and the Changing of the Guard. For a few years the solution was specific to the wheelchairs: once through Admiralty Arch at the start of The Mall, the wheelchairs were diverted left into Horse Guards Parade (where Trooping the Colour takes place). Here, a zig-zag section was introduced to make up the distance forgone by missing out The Mall and most of Birdcage Walk, and the wheelchairs rejoined the course just as Birdcage Walk became Great George Street.

It worked, but was an unsatisfactory solution, not least for missing out the crowds along The Mall.

This diversion probably also had the effect of depriving Mike Bishop of a win. In the late 1980s he was arguably the fastest man in a straight line in the country, and racing down the Mall he would have left the opposition for dead. But the multiple hairpin bends in Horse Guards Parade effectively ensured he never did win.

The solution to the problem came from changes to the main race. There was pressure from the elite athletes to have a starting time ahead of the main race. Then the elite women wanted a separate start, and an earlier starting time, so they didn't get mixed up with non-elite men and, by being separate from the elite men, their race could be seen to have its own status and validity. All of these requests could be accommodated by having a later start time for the main, "people's" race, but then there would be the issue of how long the police would allow the roads to be closed, so earlier start times it had to be. The wheelchairs also wanted a front-end start, for safety reasons ahead of all the running groups. We came in on the coat-tails of the issue, but ultimately benefitted from the solution. Rumours abounded that Jimmy Savile, purportedly in good odour with the Palace at the time, was used to approach the royal household with a request to allow The Mall to be used early enough to allow all the disparate interest groups to be accommodated. This meant altering the normal arrangements for the Changing of the Guard, which was agreed in about 1990 – I don't know the exact date – but from then on the diversion through Horse Guards Parade was abandoned. Whether Savile was actually involved as the rumours had suggested I never found out.

For some years County Hall was used as the administrative headquarters of the race, and as the medical centre at the end of the race; but the Greater London Council was abolished by Parliament in the late 1980s, the building was sold off to provide hotel accommodation, and was therefore no longer available to act as the race headquarters. And then things changed again – though not in terms of the need for staggered starts – when the course was redesigned. Now, the final few hundred yards of the race continued further along the Embankment than the original route had done. It then turned into Parliament Square, along Great George Street and Birdcage Walk, in the opposite direction from the earlier races, and swung round to the right to finish on The Mall.

Late in 1984 Mick Karaphillides and I, together with a couple of others, were funded by Stoke to go to a marathon race in Oita, in the southernmost of the main Japanese islands. The race had started in 1981 as a half-marathon, in celebration of the International Year of Disabled People, and was expanded subsequently to a full marathon. This was tough on Gordon Perry, who by then had broken 3 hours and was a few minutes faster than me. But Stoke wouldn't fund an amputee athlete, which Gordon was, and in any case Oita didn't allow single leg amputees into their race, so that was that.

Apart from experiencing a completely foreign culture, it was interesting to see the state of wheelchair design, and to hear discussions, mostly from North America but also from Europe, about possible future developments, including ideas about moving to tricycles, which within a few years was the only design available. The race was won by the French-Canadian Andre Viger in 1h 46m 21s, way faster than anything seen in Britain. Aware of how far behind we still were, in both our own times and the facilities we could offer – accommodation, transport to the start, sweep-up services and so on – we didn't issue any international invitations, beyond that to the Irish, for people to come and try London.

That perspective changed in 1987, which saw Swedish tetraplegic, Jan-Owe Matsson, taking part as a result of a private invitation from someone on our committee. The following year, either BSAD or Stoke received an invitation from Czechoslovakia to a wheelchair marathon in Brno, in southern Moravia, on the international motorcycle race-track. There was no funding, but if we could get ourselves there accommodation, food etc. would be provided. With an official invitation, we wouldn't have to change *x* pounds per day each into Czech Koruna, *and spend them*, with no option to change any underspend back at the end, nor to bring back any unspent currency, export of which was at that time a criminal offence.

So, in late August, Mick Karaphillides, Chas Sadler and I drove out to Brno. They did the race – I didn't, injured again – but the course was very hilly, quite unlike anything seen at home, with a rise and fall of a few hundred feet every lap – all 10 of them, again, quite unlike anything at home. However, one upshot of the contact was to issue an invitation to the Czechs for three or four athletes to come over to London in 1989. The winner of the Czech race, Karel Boura, was most impressive, beating both Mick and Chas handsomely, and in 1989 I was tempted to try to put a bet on him to win in London; but in the event, he didn't come over – illness – and I was careless enough not to place a bet on David Holding from East Anglia, who had come to the fore in shorter races and was available in my local bookies' at 33 to 1. He won the race, of course, the first of several victories.

None of the three Czechs produced startling times; they found the point-to-point nature of the course, without the relief afforded by the few hundred feet drop every lap, particularly hard. They didn't, I think, come again, but the Velvet Revolution occurred later that year, and there will have been many races in the West much easier for them to gain access to than London.

It was about this time that I dropped out of the organising committee altogether, just as Tanni Grey appeared on the scene in the first of her six victories. Sometimes, I watched the race on the television, and noted with approval the developments that had taken place in terms of organising a race hotel, transport to the start and from the finish, and so on. And the race did, eventually, attract the top racers from Europe, North America and the southern hemisphere – South Africa and Australia – all beyond our wildest dreams when engaged in the original battle in the early 1980s.

There was an interesting sidelight thrown on that battle from an unexpected direction. The BBC has a series of programmes called "The Reunion". Sue McGregor brings together a number of people involved in some earlier event to reminisce about how the event came to pass, what it was like to take part, what happened afterwards and so on. Amongst the events so reviewed have been the making of the film "Four Weddings and a Funeral", the Kings Cross underground station fire, and the building of the Dome at Greenwich as part of the Millennium celebrations. In about 2010 there was a programme about the creation of the London Marathon, at the end of which Sue McGregor added, "In 1983 the wheelchairs were invited in …" I thought about writing, but life's too short, and in any case the problem had long been sorted. Or so we thought…

Two matters deserve further comment. In 2013 at about 15 km into the race there was a collision between some wheelchair competitors and a female runner at a drinks station. She was Tiki Gelana, one of the elite group of women given a special start, and she was, moreover, the Olympic champion from the year before in London. Not just box office here, but in the whole of Latin America to boot. Seen from the television, this is what appeared to happen.

A group of women runners approached a drinks station. One woman (TG) detached herself from the group and moved to the right to pick up a drink – there were drinks tables on both sides of the course. At the same time, at the bottom of the screen, a group of five wheelchairs came into view, "drafting" in the way that road cyclists do. They were moving quite fast – between 15 and 20 mph, it was estimated – and my first thought was to wonder how on earth the runners could be where they were, if the wheelchairs had started in front of them. This thought was soon obliterated by the next move – the wheelchairs were running along the left- hand side of the course when TG, having found nothing to her satisfaction on the right- side table, dived across to the left to pick up a drink from there.

At the last minute – fraction of a second, actually – the wheelchairs tried to avoid hitting her. They couldn't swerve to the right, because that was where she was coming from. They couldn't speed up, because there wasn't time to put in a speed burst. There wasn't enough time for braking to have avoided a collision, so they did the only thing possible, and the natural reaction of anyone in a chair being approached suddenly from one side. They swerved in the opposite direction, to the left, just as she collided with either the third or fourth wheelchair, pushing him into the trestle tables on which all the drinks sat. Tiki Gelana herself was injured, and hobbled on until about 22 miles, when she withdrew. There was near- consternation in the commentary box about the injury she had sustained – an Olympic champion, no less! – but as far as I can remember not a word about the possible injury to Josh Cassidy, the Canadian wheelchair athlete who had won the race a few years earlier, nor about possible damage to his wheelchair (costing, as it turned out, hundreds of dollars to repair).

The problem was, of course, the front-end start for the wheelchairs, or rather the lack of it. Over 30 years from the start of the original battle, and this was still going on! From Josh Cassidy's words on the web:

"It's something I have mentioned before. I don't know who's responsible, but every year we come to overtake the women, there's 10 chairs going at 20 mph and the poor women are scrambling to find their feet. The safest thing would be to have the wheelchairs start first because one of these years a woman is going to have a leg broken, a career ruined. It's just not worth having this programme if the racers are going to suffer." Later, he tweeted:

"The wheelchairs MUST start first next year so this doesn't happen again. Was very frustrated as we have warned this was bound to happen."

Further comment seems superfluous. Except that, the following year, heed had been taken, and the wheelchairs did start first – congratulations to Hugh Brasher, Chris Brasher's son, who by now was race director. I haven't had the opportunity of talking to him about the troubles we had so long ago – it seems unlikely that Chris would have made no mention of the issue at home when it was all bubbling up. But further congratulations are in order, for in 2014 it wasn't only the wheelchairs who had their headstart. The cameras also highlighted a group of blind runners, *elite* blind runners with their guides, who were taking part in the International Paralympic Committee's (IPC) World Championship marathon race for blind athletes. And further, there was a group of elite amputee runners (leg amputees only, I think) taking part in *their* IPC-sponsored World Championship event. The congratulations are due not only to Hugh Brasher and his team for managing to accommodate the complicated arrangements that must have been necessary, but also to the IPC, who saw, and seized, the opportunity of locating their own World Championships within the framework of such a prestigious event as London. I hope Hugh Brasher's dad would have been proud.

Postscript

Notes on a few of the people who have featured to a greater or lesser extent in the story above. There are no doubt many others, of whom I have no knowledge, who played a part in getting a wheelchair section established in the Marathon.

Chris Brasher

Since dropping out of the organising group for the wheelchair event, I had no contact with him. Interestingly, at some point he switched from writing for The Observer to writing for The Sunday Times. He died in 2003, and there was a memorial service held at the "journalists' church", St Bride's in Fleet Street. For all our battles, I still think he was a great man, and I'd much rather have had him on our side from the start.

John Disley

Similarly to my lack of contact with Brasher, I had none with Disley, except once. I had been appointed by successive Sports Ministers to serve on the GB Sports Council, and subsequently the English Sports Council, between 1988 and 2001. One of the jobs I took on was to chair the Plas y Brenin Advisory Committee, a group which drew together all the users of the centre to advise the Councils on how far the centre was meeting their needs. This role continued after my formal appointment to the English Sports Council finished. In 2005 there was a celebratory dinner held at PyB to mark 50 years since it came into the ownership of the CCPR. John Disley was there, as the first senior instructor, and I was there, as chair of the PyB committee. In the crush before the sit-down dinner, the crowds parted and there was Disley, right in front of me. "Hello, John." He looked baffled, first of all – he would have had no idea how I could have come to be at such an event. But the bafflement turned rapidly to what looked like hostility: he wouldn't talk, and he turned away to find someone else to talk to. Very sad, really. He died in 2016.

Bill Parkinson

Having played such an important role in getting the Derwentwater affair going, and after taking part in the attempted canoe-camping trip in Scotland, he just disappeared from the scene. There was a rumour (there were always lots of rumours amongst those who knew him) that he had gone to America, but like the best of rumours this could be neither substantiated nor refuted.

Ivor Mitchell ("Mitch")

When I first met him, Mitch was the headmaster of a local special school in Birmingham which educated especially children with physical disabilities. He was the driving force behind a fund-raising campaign to build a swimming pool at the school, and was passionate about ensuring that the pupils from his school had worthwhile activities to do having left school, employment for some but sport and physical recreation for all. He became a vice- chairman of BSAD, and was eventually awarded an OBE for his work.

Liz Dendy

Liz was a senior officer at the GB Sports Council, whose portfolio included Women's Sport and Sport for Disabled People. She did much voluntary work in two fields, Riding for the Disabled, and the International Cerebral Palsy Sport and Recreation Association, rising to be head of each. She was awarded an MBE, and subsequently an OBE, for this work. She retired from the Sports Council in 1995.

Jenny Ward

As has already been noted, Jenny came to post-1983 meetings until she left for Switzerland in August of that year. I have had no news of her since then.

Mike O'Flynn

Mike O'Flynn just disappeared from the scene. He wasn't at the crucial April 7th meeting in County Hall, nor at the following press conference at the Waldorf; and I don't remember seeing him at/around the event itself. He must have resigned from BSAD, but I don't recall any announcement about it.

Philip Lewis

I saw Philip only once after the events described above, at a rugby match at Twickenham in about 1992.

Julia Allton
Julia was a senior lecturer in PE at Tower Hamlets Institute. She was a main organiser of the Docklands trial run in December 1982, and I first met her at the Department for Education conference in Birmingham in February 1983. She was very keen to help with the campaign, and became a kind of unofficial deputy to Jenny on the day.

Illtyd Harrington
Illtyd Harrington was originally a teacher of English. First elected to the GLC in 1964, he was deputy leader between 1973 and 1977, and then again between 1981 and 1984. We (BSAD) didn't originally write to him over the marathon business, but after our first meeting with Tony Banks and Peter Pitt, Banks' deputy, it must have been obvious to them that, as one of the Governors of the Marathon, he was high enough politically to take the case on, if he thought it worthwhile to do so. He did, and as we have seen, led the final confrontation with Brasher and Disley. He died in 2015 aged 84.

Tony Banks
Not to be confused with Tony Banks the musician from Genesis, this Tony Banks was first elected to the GLC in 1970. He was made Chair of the Arts and Recreation Committee in 1981, and it was in this capacity that we wrote to him in 1982. He was strongly in favour of the wheelchair event, but although he had been elected to the GLC before Illtyd Harrington, must have recognised the latter as having greater political clout, and hence drew him into the campaign. Subsequent to the abolition of the GLC, he was elected as MP for Newham North West in 1997, and to his astonishment was appointed Minister for Sport in 1997, a post he held for two years. He left the Commons in 2005, was appointed to a peerage, and died in 2006.

Mark Agar
Mark was the first person in this country (I think) to have completed a full, open, competitive marathon, and as such probably held the national record for a few weeks in 1981. But after the Great North Run and the Birmingham marathon later that year, he disappeared from the racing scene.

Mick Karaphillides

We first met at the 1983 Reading Half-Marathon. I never discovered the reason for his absence from the London Marathon a few weeks later, but we came across each other in different races over the next few years, notably in the British–American Marathon at Basildon later in 1983. It was in this race that Mick became the first British athlete to break 3 hours for the distance, with a time of 2h 54m; unless, that is, Gerry Kinsella had already managed to get there first (I never found out). The last encounter with Mick was when going to the marathon in Brno in September 1988.

Gerry Kinsella

In setting up the Greenbank project, Gerry was trying to offer disabled people on Merseyside the kinds of opportunities which came only late to him. There is an extensive website about the project, which offers training in IT and office skills, self-advocacy, sport and other topics concerned with improving the life chances of disabled people in what at times must seem a distinctly unfriendly, if not downright hostile, world. To those looking at Liverpool from the outside, his fundraising efforts seemed to involve the whole of Merseyside. He gained the wholesale support of the "Two Bishops" – the Catholic Derek Worlock and the Anglican David Sheppard – and continued fund-raising for many years, including repeating the Land's End–John o'Groats trip in 1989 with Vince Ross – in a tandem, articulated fore-and-aft wheelchair built by Vince especially for the event. He was awarded an MBE for his work creating the Greenbank centre.

Philip Craven

Injured in a climbing accident at the age of only 16, Philip was already a seasoned wheelchair basketball international when, aged 22, he wrote to me in hospital. In the 1990s Sports 'n Spokes selected their world's best-ever team, and he was one of the five chosen. Awarded an MBE for his basketball prowess, he rose to become Secretary, and then Chairman, of the International Wheelchair Basketball Federation. Further achievements saw him become President of the International Paralympic Committee (retired 2017), the "disabled" equiv-alent of the International Olympic Committee, in 2002, joining the IOC as a full member in 2003, and being awarded a knighthood in 2005. It's a long way from falling out of a wheelchair in Heidelberg.

Lightning Source UK Ltd.
Milton Keynes UK
UKOW01f1309090218
317587UK00001B/88/P

9 781912 262571